Christian Devotional for Women with Relatable Bible Verses

FLOURISH IN LIFE LOVED BY JESUS

LISA WILT

Christian Devotional for Women with Relatable Bible Verses
Flourish in Life Loved by Jesus

Copyright© 2025 by Lisa Wilt at
Rx For The Soulful Heart

ISBN 979-8-9892416-2-0 All rights reserved.
No part of this book may be reproduced in any form or by any electronic or mechanical means, including information storage and retrieval systems, without written permission from the author.

All Scripture quotations are taken from:

- Holy Bible, New Living Translation, copyright ©1996, 2004, 2007, 2013, 2015 by Tyndale House Foundation. Used by permission of Tyndale House Publishers, Inc., Carol Stream, Illinois 60188. All rights reserved or
- Those passages denoted with (MSG) are taken from The Message, copyright © 1993, 1994, 1995, 1996, 2000, 2001, 2002 by Eugene H. Peterson. Used by permission of NavPress. All rights reserved. Represented by Tyndale House Publishers, Inc.
- Scriptures with (KJV) are taken from the KING JAMES VERSION: KING JAMES VERSION, public domain.

To:

From:

Date:

Acknowledgments

Sue Steen: As my long-time friend and new-found Pickleball partner, I am exceedingly grateful for your editing expertise. You are an exemplary team player. Your willingness to serve with excellence both on and off the court inspires me.

Sharon Tate M.Div.: You lost your home to fire, but you never lost your fire to inspire others to walk by faith. Thank you for editing this manuscript to insure Biblical accuracy. While I appreciate your expertise, I am most grateful for your friendship.

Sharon Baker: You are the most incredible Godmother to my children. When Alyssa was a child, she introduced you as her "fairy godmother." She chose the most enchanting title she could imagine! You continue to inspire us all as "The Crazy Goat Lady," celebrated around the world for your compassionate work distributing goats through World Vision. I am deeply grateful for your help editing.

Introduction

You were made to FLOURISH! Because you need more than caffeine or carbs, this new daily devotional for women is fueled with the most potent encouragement imaginable—God's triumphant promises.

You need rest to FLOURISH! Because resting in God's assuring, all-powerful, audacious love completes you, catapults your confidence, and quiets the voice in your head that whispers you are not enough.

You need time to FLOURISH! Because your time is a valuable gift, these simple devotions include a relatable Bible verse, uplifting thought or story, and free space to journal.

You need God's help to FLOURISH! Because you are treasured and God longs to hear from you, each devotion ends with an inspiring prayer.

You're irresistible when you FLOURISH! Because you are perfectly understood and completely loved by Christ, you radiate His light and warmth, attracting others.

NOURISH *your faith in bold, new ways and:*

- quiet the voice in your head that causes you to doubt yourself and rest in God's confident assurance that you are *more than enough.*
- live fabulously fulfilled and fearless, grateful for every gift.
- experience genuine JOY with The Holy Spirit as your personal Trainer, Comforter, and Friend.
- worry less, pray more and sleep well

Flawed yet Flourishing

> We are the clay, and you are the potter.
> We all are formed by your hand.
> Isaiah 64:8

If you've ever felt like you're less than enough, you're not alone. I, too, wrestle with feelings of inadequacy. That's why the story of the cracked pot deeply resonates with me. Here's a brief retelling:

A water-bearer in India carried two large pots, one hanging on each end of a pole balanced across his neck. One pot was perfect, delivering a full portion of water each day. The other had a crack and always arrived half full. The cracked pot, much like me at times, felt convinced it was a failure. One day, it confessed to the water-bearer: *"I am so ashamed of my flaw. Because of this crack, I can only deliver half my load. Your efforts are wasted because of me."* The water-bearer, a beautiful representation of our Creator, responded: *"Did you notice the flowers along your side of the path? I planted seeds there, knowing of your flaw. Each day, as we walked, you watered them. Without your crack, there would be no flourishing flowers."*[1] This story reminds me that our perceived imperfections are not burdens to bear, but opportunities for God to work through us. He uses even what we see as flaws to bring beauty and life.

How might God use your perceived weaknesses to encourage others?

Prayer to flourish: Lord Jesus, you know my flaws and how easily I succumb to the lies of the Accuser, believing I am not enough. Thank You for loving me as I am, imperfections and all. I trust that You can use my weaknesses to create something beautiful in the lives of others. Help me to flourish and bring glory to Your name. Amen.

---

1. https://bible.org/illustration/cracked-pot (accessed 12/15/23)

A Flourishing Life

> Give away your life; you'll find life given back,
> but not merely given back—given back with bonus and blessing.
> Giving, not getting, is the way.
> Luke 6:38 (MSG)

I love free gifts and unexpected bonuses. Today's verse feels like both—an extraordinary invitation to a life that overflows. Generosity, it turns out, is the secret ingredient. Life seldom unfolds according to plan. There are hardships.

As a high school student, I dreamed of becoming a writer, while my father envisioned me as a pharmacist. I served in pharmacy for nearly 35 years. Now in retirement I am writing.

In His perfect timing, God beautifully allowed my dream of writing to flourish. Perhaps your life, too, looks different from what you once imagined. Over the decades, I've learned an important truth—dreams don't truly thrive when we focus solely on our own goals. Real growth begins when we align our lives with God's priorities. He upends the wisdom of the world: to rise is to lift others, to flourish is to help others thrive.

Scripture repeatedly reflects this kingdom principle. Elijah passed his mantle to Elisha. Moses entrusted his staff to Joshua. Rahab sheltered spies. Elizabeth encouraged Mary. Barnabas poured into Paul, who in turn mentored Timothy. Each act of selfless giving demonstrates that God's way is not about grasping but offering. It's in giving that we discover life abundant and hearts aligned with His purpose.

What little dreams might become big realities if you were to dream big and give generously?

_____

_____

_____

Prayer to flourish: King of Kings, Your kingdom operates so differently from the ways of the world. Thank You for teaching me to live generously and for blessing me in ways I cannot always see or understand. Amen.

Planting Promises, Uprooting Worry

Fix your thoughts on what is true, and honorable, and right, and pure, and lovely, and admirable. Think about things that are excellent and worthy of praise.

Philippians 4:8b

You may have heard the whimsical rhyme: "Your mind is a garden. Your thoughts are the seeds. You can grow flowers, or you can grow weeds."[1] Easy to read but hard to live. Why do my thoughts drift to the weedy worst over the fragrant good? Why do we let worry steal our joy?

This is a hard question without an easy answer. In looking for ways to worry less, I've found it helps to start every day with a promise from God's Word. Nestled in its 66 books it's estimated there are over 3,500 promises in the Bible.[2] That's a new promise every day for nearly a decade before circling back to Genesis. Our Bible verse today is one of my life mottos. It keeps worry at bay and helps me focus my mind and time on what truly matters. It even guides my choices about what I read, watch, and listen to.

Both faith and fear demand we believe in something. We have a choice each day. So if our mind is a garden and our thoughts are the seeds, let's intentionally grow flowers instead of weeds.

Like flowers what thoughts bring you joy? What worrisome thoughts need Weed-B-Gon®?

_____

_____

_____

Prayer to flourish: Lord, please help me make wise decisions about what my eyes see, what fills my mind and becomes my focus. I want to magnify You and minimize worry. In Jesus' name, Amen.

1. Author unknown
2. https://www.bibleinfo.com/en/questions/how-many-bible-promises-are-there (accessed 7/14/22)

Grace Feels Like Comfy Jeans

> No one puts new wine into old wineskins. For the new wine would burst the wineskins, spilling the wine and ruining the skins. New wine must be stored in new wineskins.
>
> Luke 5:37-38

I started the day in a bit of a funk because my jeans were too tight, and my to-do list was too long. That's when Jesus, in His perfect timing, dropped the mic with a message of grace through today's reading. I'd read the passage many times before, but it had never touched me—probably because I've never owned a wineskin.

My Bible's study notes reminded me that wineskins were made from goatskins sewn together at the edges to form watertight bags, much like modern-day canteens. In Jesus' day wine was often safer to drink than water. Since new wine expands as it ferments, it had to be stored in new wineskins. Old, rigid, inflexible wineskins didn't expand and could burst.

Suddenly, sitting in my too-tight jeans, the metaphor clicked in a fresh way. These old jeans, like old wineskins, didn't expand with me and now felt as if they could burst. In that moment I understood clearly: old wineskins—and old jeans—mirror the old covenant of laws from the Old Testament. Rigid and unyielding, they excluded rather than embraced.

The new covenant of grace in the New Testament feels like my stretchy, comfy jeans. Grace stretches, covering my flaws rather than pointing them out. Grace covers me in love so I can love others. Everybody needs a pair of comfy jeans and everybody needs loving grace.

How might you extend grace to someone today?

_____

_____

_____

Prayer to flourish: Jesus, thank you for s-t-r-e-t-c-h-i-n-g my thinking by showing me what loving grace looks like. I don't need to fit into my skinny jeans, look perfect, or accomplish great things to receive your love. Thank You for Your grace—especially on mornings when I'm frustrated or in a funk. Amen.

The Present

> God saved you by his grace when you believed. And you can't take
> credit for this; it is a gift from God. Salvation is not
> a reward for the good things we have done,
> so none of us can boast about it.
> Ephesians 2:8-9

I love the saying, "Yesterday is history. Tomorrow is a mystery, but today is a *gift*. That's why it's called *the present*."[1]

If you were to give a gift to a friend, but they never opened it, how would you feel? I would wonder if I had offended them and would question myself and my gift giving. Did they think it a lousy gift? Did they understand that I want them to enjoy it?

Today's reading refers to God's most precious gift—Jesus, who offers us the gift of salvation. This gift isn't earned by our deeds; it's freely given out of God's grace. When we accept Jesus into our hearts, eternity doesn't begin someday in heaven—it begins in the here and now. Salvation is a gift for today, bringing us joy, peace, and the assurance that we are loved.

God wants us to enjoy Christ and to live in confident assurance every day. Time won't be hurried or halted. Every moment is a gift. Let's open it together over the coming days!

Since the present is a gift, what do you most enjoy about the present? What do you least enjoy about the present?

_____

_____

_____

Prayer to flourish: Lord, more than any other group of people, as Christians we have the ultimate gift money can't buy. Thank you for the gift of eternity that is meant for today. Help me to unwrap each day in joyful expectancy. I am grateful for Your present of today and Your promise of heaven. Amen.

---

1. https://quotes.yourdictionary.com/author/eleanor-roosevelt/620985 (accessed 7/3/22)

Dad's Big Shoes

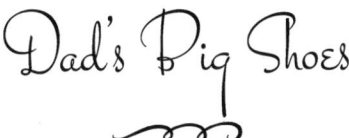

*I know what I'm doing. I have it all planned out—plans to take care
of you, not abandon you, plans to give you the future you hope for.
When you call on me, when you come and pray to me, I'll listen.
When you come looking for me, you'll find me.*
Jeremiah 29:11-13 (MSG)

Dads have big spiritual shoes to fill. Even if your dad has small feet, his spiritual shoes are enormous, as earthly fathers are the visible image of our invisible Heavenly Father. The Bible tells us that all creation points to our Creator.[1]

If your earthly father was loving, kind, and attentive, you'll likely see these qualities in your Heavenly Father. But if your earthly dad was unloving, unkind, and inattentive, you may see God as unloving, unkind, and inattentive.

My friend, please know that your Heavenly Father loves you unconditionally. He is watching over you, and Jesus is interceding for you at this very moment.[2] Our Bible reading today assures us that He wants to bless you and has good plans for you, plans to prosper you and give you the future you hope for. Our Heavenly Father fills more than big shoes, He fulfills all our needs according to His riches in glory.[3] His love is perfect, unwavering, and eternal.

How do you envision our Heavenly Father?

_____

_____

_____

Prayer to flourish: Lord, help me to relate to You better. I see You now through the lens of my earthly father, but I know You are so much bigger and better. Thank You for the promise of eternity to better know You and understand the depth of Your love. Most of all, thank You for Your mercy each day. I look forward to the promise of heaven. Amen.

---

1. Romans 1:20
2. Philippians 4:19
3. Philippians 4:19

Second Chances

*Where is another God like you,
who pardons the guilt of the remnant,
overlooking the sins of his special people?
You will not stay angry with your people forever,
because you delight in showing unfailing love.*
Micah 7:18

We may never have a second chance to make a first impression...except with God. I'm so grateful that our Father is the God of second chances. He looks beyond our past and sees our future. He sees what we can become. Want proof? The Bible gives us plenty of examples beyond today's reading.

Jonah was an unwilling whale rider, yet God chose him to deliver a whale of a message saving the entire nation of Nineveh.[1] Moses was a long-time stutterer, yet God chose him to stand up and speak up for the enslaved Hebrew nation.[2] And then there was Paul—a proud know-it-all who God blinded, so that the world could see more clearly through his writings.[3] God doesn't define us by our failures. While others may see the baggage of our past, God sees through it to the beauty of our potential. He is the God of second chances, the God who rewrites our stories with His unfailing love.

Who have you wanted to give you a second chance? How might you give someone a second chance today?

_____

_____

_____

Prayer to flourish: Lord Jesus, thank You for giving me second chances. Please help me to extend that same grace to others and look beyond their outward appearance. Open my eyes to focus not on what they have done in the past but what they can do in the future. Thank you for giving me Your ability to see the best in others. Amen.

---

1. Jonah 1-3
2. Exodus 4-14
3. Acts 9

Greener Grass

> Love doesn't want what it doesn't have.
> 1 Corinthians 13: 4a (MSG)

We've all done it. Sometimes we don't even realize we are doing it because we do it so often. We envy others. We covet what they have and are jealous. We look at their relationships and think the grass is greener on their side of the fence. But creation tells us the grass doesn't grow greener on one side. Rather, the grass is greener wherever it has been watered.

Envy is easy. Watering our own relationships and faith is hard. I've found that, for me, envy is like crabgrass. It can ruin my lawn and my life if left unchecked.

So how do we get rid of envy? We sow seeds of gratefulness. Then we water it with generosity toward others. We are grateful for our family and tell them how much we appreciate them. We give to them and others.

We *love* them even when we don't *like* them. We don't keep score of their sins. We don't revel with "I-told-you-so's." We want what's best for them, not what they deserve. We extend mercy and grace. Today's reading reminds us that loving others like Jesus results in lives that are greener no matter what side of the fence we live on.

Whose life seems perfect?
How do you feel toward them?

_____

_____

_____

Prayer to flourish: Lord, it's easy to envy but it's hard to love. Help me to be patient when I'm tired. Kind when I'm irritable. Humble rather than hateful. Grateful and content rather than demanding and unhappy. Thank you for every blade in my lawn and person in my life. Amen.

Chiaroscuro and a Time for Everything

For everything there is a season, a time for every activity under heaven. A time to be born and a time to die. A time to plant and a time to harvest. A time to cry and a time to laugh. A time to grieve and a time to dance. A time to scatter stones and a time to gather stones. A time to tear and a time to mend.
A time to be quiet and a time to speak.
Ecclesiastes 3:1, 2, 4, 7

Is it just me or do you sometimes experience entire seasons in a single day? I'm simultaneously in a season of grieving, as I buried my dad, and a season of dancing, as I babysit my first grandchild. I've found it's time to be quiet as my grown children find their own way, and a time to speak up as my husband and I forge new pathways in retirement.

Grieving and dancing. Tears and laughter. Silence and speaking. These are the seasons I experienced just this morning.

A life beautifully lived–just as a portrait beautifully painted–has both light and dark tones creating contrast and depth. In art this is called *chiaroscuro*. Leonardo da Vinci developed *chiaroscuro* and perfected it in his world-famous painting, The Mona Lisa.[1] Our God is the ultimate artist, bending both shadows and light into exquisite art. He uses dark trials to create depth to our character. He uses light to create inspiring beauty. We are His masterpiece.

What joyful moments have you experienced dancing between moments of deep grief?

_____

_____

_____

Prayer to flourish: Creator God, thank You for making my life a masterpiece. I don't like dark days, but I know You use them to create beauty, like a master artist who paints using *chiaroscuro*. Amen.

---

1. https://www.britannica.com/art/chiaroscuro (accessed 6/6/24)

I'll Fix It!

Let us run with endurance the race God has set before us. We do this by keeping our eyes on Jesus, the champion who initiates and perfects our faith.
Hebrews 12:1b-2

I still smile when I remember how my confident toddler swaggered into his bedroom one evening as my husband was putting together his "big boy bed." He didn't have command of the English language but took command of the situation waving for his dad to, "Move out the way. I fix it!"

Garrett's cocky confidence makes me wonder how often God looks at me and smiles when I think I can do everything on my own. Sometimes I even tell God how to fix things as if I know best.

Martha did this when she stormed out of the kitchen to inform Jesus just how He should correct Mary for not helping her. The disciples followed suit when they suggested that Jesus send the crowd away because feeding them would cost too much.

When we try to fix things ourselves, we often make a mess. But when we fix our eyes on Jesus, He can fix any mess. Sometimes Jesus answers our prayers with a better solution than we could have imagined or sought.

When have you told Jesus exactly how to answer your prayers to fix a situation? When has He answered your prayers with a better solution?

_____

_____

_____

Prayer to flourish: Lord, thank You for always listening, even when I pray cocky prayers as if I am all-knowing and am better equipped than You to understand the situation. Like a toddler, I have much to learn. Please grant me wisdom. I love You. Amen.

Yesterday's Gratitude and Today's Blessings

> I'm thanking you, God, from a full heart,
> I'm writing the book on your wonders.
> I'm whistling, laughing, and jumping for joy;
> I'm singing your song, High God.
> Psalm 9:1-2 (MSG)

Here's an eye-opening thought: What if we woke up this morning with only those things we remembered to thank God for yesterday? It's a sobering question that could transform how we live each day. This idea reminds me of the movie *Groundhog Day*, where a jaded TV weatherman finds himself reliving the same day over and over until he finally learns to live it right.[1] Imagine if a movie were made about our lives, with the twist that we only woke up with the things we had expressed gratitude for the day before. Would it change how you and I approach life? I think it would.

Today's reading is focused on gratitude and the joy that flows from a thankful heart. In my own life I've found gratitude is the secret sauce for a big, happy life. Paul says it this way in Philippians 4:12-13, "I've learned by now to be quite content whatever my circumstances. I'm just as happy with little as with much, with much as with little. I've found the recipe for being happy whether full or hungry, hands full or hands empty. Whatever I have, wherever I am, I can make it through anything in the One who makes me who I am." Gratitude shifts our focus away from what we lack and opens our eyes to what we already have. It's the daily choice to live in awareness of God's blessings, big and small, and to find joy in recognizing His hand in our lives.

When do you find gratitude hardest?

_____

_____

_____

Prayer to flourish: Jehovah Jireh, You are my Provider. Thank You for the big blessings and the small ones. Open my eyes and my heart to find extraordinary joy tucked between ordinary moments. I am grateful for yesterday. I trust You for today. And I hope in You for tomorrow. Amen.

---

1. https://www.imdb.com/title/tt0107048/ (accessed 6/29/24)

A Common Man with Uncommon Kindness

'Now which of these three would you say was a neighbor to the man who was attacked by bandits?' Jesus asked.
The man replied, 'The one who showed him mercy.'
Then Jesus said, 'Yes, now go and do the same.'
Luke 10:36-37

Remember the story Jesus told about *The Good Samaritan* who helped the man who was robbed, stripped naked, beaten, and left to die? Both the religious leader (a priest) and the religious person (a Levite from God's chosen people) left him half dead in the ditch. Jesus chose a common man (a Samaritan enemy) to show uncommon kindness.

The Samaritan likely knew all too well what it felt like to be mistreated and disliked. Perhaps you know that feeling too. Maybe you haven't been physically attacked, but you've been ripped off by a scammer. Perhaps your dreams were shattered by someone who broke their promises or forsook their vows. Maybe, while spared from physical abuse, you've endured the pain of emotional or verbal wounds. Sometimes, those we expect to care—like spiritual leaders or friends in the faith—look the other way, leaving us feeling abandoned. But here's the beautiful truth: Jesus sees you. He knows your pain, and He calls each of us to extend kindness and mercy to our neighbors.

But who is our neighbor? Sometimes, it's the elderly person next door who craves conversation when we feel busiest. Maybe it's a mother-in-law living far away, feeling left out and longing for connection. Perhaps it's someone we've never met before—a stranger waiting in the grocery store line alongside us. Every common moment carries an opportunity to show uncommon kindness.

Who has surprised you with uncommon kindness?

_____

_____

_____

Prayer to flourish: Lord, please give me courage to step out in faith. Open my eyes to see opportunities to show common kindness. Thank You for Your uncommon kindness. Amen.

The Only Sermon Jesus Ever Wrote

"Teacher," they said to Jesus, "this woman was caught in the act of adultery. The law of Moses says to stone her. What do you say?" They were trying to trap him into saying something they could use against him, but Jesus stooped down and wrote in the dust with his finger. They kept demanding an answer, so he stood up again and said, "All right, but let the one who has never sinned throw the first stone!" Then he stooped down again and wrote in the dust.

John 8:4-8

Truth becomes hard if it's not softened by love; love becomes soft if it's not strengthened by truth. While the origin of this saying may be unclear, Jesus lived it out perfectly. He spoke truth in love, meeting people right where they were but never leaving them there. Instead, He inspired them to rise higher, as seen in His gentle yet firm words, *"Go and sin no more."* It was the perfect balance—unconditional yet uncompromising, tender yet resolute. Stooping down in love, yet standing tall in truth. In today's reading, we see this balance powerfully illustrated in the story of the woman caught in the act of adultery. Paraded before Him by her accusers, she faced not just judgment but potential death. Jesus, however, did something unexpected. He stooped down and wrote in the dirt. What He wrote, we may never know—His only written "sermon" remains a mystery. But whatever it was, it pierced the hearts of her accusers. One by one, they left until none remained. Then, Jesus turned to the woman and asked, *"Where are your accusers? Didn't even one of them condemn you?"* When she replied, *"No, Lord,"* Jesus spoke words of both grace and truth: *"Neither do I. Go and sin no more."* This moment encapsulates the heart of Jesus—a perfect blend of love and truth. His words remind us that we are seen, valued, and lovingly called to live a life transformed by His truth.

How might love soften your words as a wife, mother, daughter, or friend?

Prayer to flourish: Jesus, You are the perfect balance of love and truth. Your truth is softened by love, and Your love is strengthened by truth. Please help me to become more like You and stand in love, not judgement. Amen.

What We've Heard

> He (God) doesn't treat us as our sins deserve, nor pay us back in full for our wrongs. As high as heaven is over the earth, so strong is his love to those who fear him. And as far as sunrise is from sunset, he has separated us from our sins.
> Psalm 103:10-12 (MSG)

My dad used to say, "Gossip is cheap." Yet so often, we find ourselves disliking people based on what we've heard about them. This thought made me pause and reflect: God knows every tarnished thought I've ever had, every angry word I've spoken and every mistake I've made. And yet, He doesn't dislike me. He loves me—unconditionally.

God is truly on our side. Our Bible reading today reminds us of His incredible love, a love so vast that He has tossed our sins as far away as the sunrise is from the sunset. This truth fills me with peace.

What if, instead of disliking others based on rumors or assumptions, we chose to extend the same mercy and grace that God lavishes on us? With The Holy Spirit's help, we can give people the benefit of the doubt and love them as God loves us. This is mercy in action.

Matthew 5:7 reassures us: *"Blessed are the merciful, for they shall receive mercy."* God offers us new mercies every morning. In turn, we are called to bless others—both through our words and our deeds—reflecting His love in all we do.

When do you find it hardest not to gossip?
When have you been hurt by gossip?

_____

_____

_____

Prayer to flourish: Jesus, so many bad things have been said about You. As Christians (or little Christs) help us to represent You well so that others want to know You personally. Thank You for forgiving me when I fall short, acting and speaking in ways that hurt others. Amen.

Facial Recognition & Self-Talk

*What matters is not your outer appearance—
the styling of your hair, the jewelry you wear, the cut of your
clothes—but your inner disposition. Cultivate inner beauty,
the gentle, gracious kind that God delights in.*
1 Peter 3:3-4 (MSG)

When my phone's facial recognition can't identify me, I jump to the conclusion that I must really look bad. Thinking the worst about myself, I fixate on my imperfections. But when my husband's phone doesn't recognize him, Dave doesn't overthink it, because he knows that technology has glitches.

While men and women each process information differently, we each can give self-doubt and concerns about flaws too much mental real estate. Both beauty and strength are fleeting, and neither defines our worth.

That's when simple truths like those found in today's reading help reassure and refocus me. Being gentle, gracious, and kind is ageless and attracts others to Christ. Instead of internalizing negative thoughts, this helps me focus on the more important positive traits I can possess when I walk with The Holy Spirit.

How much time do you spend focusing on your physical flaws, trying to cover them? How much time do you spend on nurturing your spiritual gifts?

_____

_____

_____

Prayer to flourish: Lord, please help me prioritize so I am more focused on those characteristics and activities that have lasting affects and less focused on fading beauty. You remind me that faith, hope, and love last forever, and the greatest of these is love.[1] **Let my inner beauty and love for others be ever-increasing and undeniable as I shine, pointing others toward you. Amen.**

---

1. 1 Corinthians 13:13

GPS

> By your words I can see where I'm going;
> they throw a beam of light on my dark path.
> I've committed myself and I'll never turn back
> from living by your righteous order.
> Everything's falling apart on me, God;
> put me together again with your Word.
> Psalm 119:105-107 (MSG)

"You have arrived." We've all heard our GPS tell us we've arrived only to look around and wonder: "What? Where am I? This isn't where I want to be." If I'm honest, this also happens to me spiritually, and there is a discrepancy between what others see—"You have arrived"—and what I see.

Especially when I feel disconnected from God, I look critically at myself, my family, and my house. Outwardly, it might seem like I've achieved a measure of success or happiness, but inwardly, my current reality often looks nothing like I envisioned.

This is when I realize how much I need a Savior—not just to save me from my circumstances but to save me from myself. I need His Spirit—my personal Trainer, my Comforter, my Counselor, my Helper, and my Friend. Unlike the ever-changing systems of GPS technology, prone to errors and updates, God's Spirit is steadfast. Hebrews 13:8 reminds us: *"Jesus Christ is the same yesterday, today, and forever."* His ways are perfect, and He never leads us astray.

In what areas of your life do you need direction?

_____

_____

_____

Prayer to flourish: God, You are the Alpha and the Omega, the beginning and the end. Sometimes I feel like I am at the end of my rope and I don't know what to do next. Thank You for always being with me, especially when I find myself feeling stranded, confused, or lost. I love You, Lord, and while I sometimes make the wrong turn, I know You are always with me. Amen.

The Blessed Exchange: Giving Over Worry

> Give all your worries and cares to God,
> for he cares about you.
> 1 Peter 5:7

At 3:00 a.m. I found myself staring at the ceiling, replaying an interaction with a friend, consumed with worry over why she responded the way she did. Worry has a way of creeping into our hearts and minds, magnifying our struggles and diminishing our view of God's steadfast care.

But here's a powerful truth: if you've mastered worry, you already know how to meditate. Worry is dwelling on fears. Meditation, however, is dwelling on God's promises. What you dwell on shapes your heart. If you shift your focus from fear to faith, you'll unlock the transforming power of prayerful meditation.

Fixating on our own struggles only leads to anxiety. But when we turn outward—actively seeking ways to bless others—we step into a new rhythm of grace. In giving, we receive. In encouraging others, we are uplifted. In serving, we are blessed. God's design is breathtaking in its simplicity: as we empty ourselves, He fills us with His peace.

Together, let's release our worries to God and invite Him to replace them with opportunities to bless someone in need.

What worries weigh heaviest during this season of life?

_____

_____

_____

Prayer to flourish: Prince of Peace, I give my worries to You, trusting in Your care. Replace my anxieties with Your peace. Help me shift my focus to blessing others, knowing Your love flows through me. May Your presence fill my heart with faith, and may Your peace guard my thoughts. Amen.

Our Internal Antidepressant

You'll not likely go wrong here if you keep remembering that our Master said, "You're far happier giving than getting."
Acts 20:35 (MSG)

Jesus wasn't joking when He said it was better to give than receive.[1] This age-old paradox is hard to believe, so modern-day scientists decided to study it. When patients were put in an MRI scanner and told they would be giving some of their money to charity, you might think they would be alarmed. But no! The areas of their brains associated with pleasure lit up like a freshman wallflower being asked to prom by the senior quarterback.

Why does this happen? Giving to others triggers the release of dopamine—a neurotransmitter that exists to promote happiness. It helps us move through life. Dopamine is our own internal antidepressant. This reminds us that generosity doesn't just bless others; it blesses us too.

Jesus had a way of saying things simply. What has taken scientists years to study and me multiple paragraphs to say only took Jesus six Greek words: "It's better to give than receive."[2]

When have you found joy in giving?

Prayer to flourish: Maker of the Universe, sometimes I hold so tightly to what I have that I forget the difference between ownership and stewardship. You are the Giver of all gifts. I am Your steward. Everything could be gone in an instant. Thank You for blessing me. Please help me to become a blessing to others. Amen.

---

1. Acts 20:35
2. Acts 20:35b. "Μακάριόν ἐστιν μᾶλλον διδόναι ἢ λαμβάνειν." The Greek translation of "It's better to give than receive.

Imperfect People

> "For the mountains may move and the hills disappear,
> but even then my faithful love for you will remain.
> My covenant of blessing will never be broken,"
> says the Lord, who has mercy on you.
> Isaiah 54:10

Religious people sometimes give the church a bad name. Can I get an amen? If you've been hurt by those who claim to represent God, you and me and Jesus have this in common. Jesus was despised by religious leaders. They questioned Him, misrepresented Him, rejected Him, ridiculed Him, and plotted revenge on Him.

They were so jealous, they paid to have Him betrayed, falsely charged, then crucified by their Roman enemy. They rejoiced when

He was dead. But that's not the end of Jesus' story, and it's only the beginning of ours.

Today's Scripture reminds us that there is nothing we can do to lose God's love. We learn that His covenant blessing will never be withdrawn. Our Father understands that the world is full of flawed people who hurt others. There is no perfect church because the church is made of imperfect people. Yet, even in the midst of brokenness, we have a perfect Savior who loves us perfectly. His love knows no end.[1]

Have you been hurt by someone who was religious?

Prayer to flourish: Lord, I love You, but it's sometimes hard to love Your people because they are unkind. I'm so grateful that You can relate to being hurt by people who should know better. Please heal my heart. Help me to see that all Christians are not hypocrites. Help me to look for, find, and experience the good among Your imperfect people. Amen.

---

1. Lamentations 3:22, Psalm 36:5,7, 9-10.

The Missing Cuff Link

Joyful are those who listen to me.
Proverbs 8:34a

The hunt was on before our annual black-tie banquet. My husband, crawling on the bedroom carpet in his tuxedo, was searching for his missing cuff link. Moments earlier both cuff links had been safely on his nightstand.

Meanwhile, I stood in front of the bathroom mirror, carefully styling my hair while trying not to smudge my freshly-painted nails. I felt a little extra fancy in my new evening gown—an absolute bargain at $19.99! (Score!) That's when my toddler tugged at my dress and then her ear, whimpering, "Caught, Mommy."

And there it was—Dave's elusive cuff link perfectly lodged in her ear. With a steady hand and a trusty pair of eyebrow tweezers, I retrieved it, and we made it to the fancy fundraiser just in time.

On the drive over, I reflected on today's Scripture, which I had read earlier: *"Joyful are those who listen to me."* Seven simple words, yet incredibly challenging to live out. Life gets noisy—filled with carpools, caregiving, cooking, and cleaning. Sometimes I realize I need to spiritually remove "cuff links" that block my ears, keeping me from truly hearing God.

Today's verse reminds me that joy and listening to God are intimately connected. I know I could use more joy. Yet, I often struggle to carve out quiet time with Him amid my loud, chaotic days of kiddos and crises. Opening my Bible and quieting my heart to listen with my spirit is a daily challenge—but oh, the joy that comes when I let Him speak.

When do you most struggle to be joyful and peaceful?

_____

_____

_____

Prayer to flourish: Jesus, some days I struggle, feeling stressed, and joy seems a world away. Thank You for teaching me today that joy is linked to listening. Help me listen to You through Your Word, creation, Godly teachers, Christian music, and The Holy Spirit's still small voice. Reveal to me new ways to hear you. I want to listen with my heart. Amen.

Twirling Teeter Totters

Look, God's home is now among his people! He will live with them, and they will be his people. God himself will be with them. He will wipe every tear from their eyes, and there will be no more death or sorrow or crying or pain. All these things are gone forever.
And the one sitting on the throne said,
"Look, I am making everything new!"
Revelation 21:1b-5a (emphasis mine)

We each have fond memories of the backyard we grew up in. For me, the highlight was the teeter-totter—one that not only went up and down but also twirled around. Like everything else in our yard, my dad made it from salvaged materials. He was incredibly creative and resourceful, turning old, worn-out things into something new and fun for all the neighborhood kids to enjoy.

To this day I love finding ways to repurpose old things into something fresh and meaningful. It brings me joy—and it reminds me of our heavenly Father. He, too, specializes in making all things new, including us. He created us, so He knows the unique talents and gifts we possess. When we use those gifts to bless others, He multiplies them, allowing us to share even more. Blessings, like boomerangs, always come back around.

What you may see as an ordinary skill becomes extraordinary when placed in God's hands. Whatever talents or treasures you and I have can be used for His glory—to bless those around us, whether they're up, down, or all around us. With God, nothing goes to waste, and everything has the potential to become something beautiful.

What could you repurpose to make new to bring joy to others?

_____

_____

_____

Prayer to flourish: Creator God, thank You for Your promise to make all things new. Somedays I feel old and worn out. Please help me to be resourceful with the gifts You have given me, to use them for Your glory to bring others joy, drawing them to you. Amen.

Man of Sorrow & Joy

> I (Jesus) came so they can have real and eternal life,
> more and better life than they ever dreamed of.
> John 10:10b (MSG)

We often think of Jesus as a man of sorrows. But make no mistake, He was also a man of great joy. Without wavering, Jesus shares His life's motto, proclaiming in today's Scripture that He came to give us a better life than we have ever dreamed of.

Jesus liked parties. His first miracle debuted during a party where ordinary water became extraordinary wine. He was criticized for eating and drinking when those in positions of power thought He should be fasting not feasting. He befriended and defended the least and the lost. Our High Priest had friends in low places.

He loved to hang out with wonder-loving kiddos who loved to hang all over Him. He looked for the good in others even when they were known for doing bad.

He offered compassion to a Samaritan stranger in the heat of the day instead of giving her the cold shoulder. He welcomed shady tax collectors instead of shunning them. Jesus made Sundays fun days, setting aside heavy rules for light meals with hungry followers. With Jesus we can experience true joy even amidst sorrow. His joy is abundant, His love is unshakable, and His presence brings life and peace.

What brings you heavenly joy?
Why not do more of that!

_____

_____

_____

Prayer to flourish: Precious Jesus, I invite You into my life. Please open my eyes to see Your wonder, to experience Your peace and to overflow with Your life-affirming love. I want to model Your joy and share it like ice cream on a hot day. Amen.

Nourish and Flourish

> Kind words heal and help;
> cutting words wound and maim.
> Proverbs 15:4 (MSG)

Compliments and criticism are much like sunlight and rain—both nourish growth. While I tend to favor the warmth of compliments, there's a delicate balance to maintain. According to the *Harvard Business Review*, the ideal ratio is five compliments for every one critique. As a spouse and parent, this prompts me to pause: Do my words embody this balance within my home?

Too much sunlight can scorch a plant, while too much rain can drown it. In the same way, well-intentioned critiques can overwhelm those I love if they come in excess. I'm reminded of the wise saying: *"When people praise you, don't let it go to your head, and when they criticize you, don't let it get to your heart."* Still, I confess this is easier said than done.

Our reading today delivers a vivid reminder of the power of our words. Sharp, cutting remarks can shatter friendships, weaken marriages, and leave lasting scars on children and siblings. In contrast, kind and healing words can restore, uplift, and nourish the soul.

How might your words bring healing and help to those closest to you? Where can you balance truth with kindness in your conversations?

_____

_____

_____

Prayer to flourish: El Roi, You are the God who sees. You see how words hurt and maim. And You also see how words can heal and help. Please open my eyes to see characteristics that are compliment worthy. When I do deliver criticisms, please help me to speak with kindness. Help me to speak true words that are softened by love and loving words that are strengthened by truth. Amen.

Justified Until Proven Otherwise

Knowing that a man is not justified by the works of the law, but by the faith of Jesus Christ, even we have believed in Jesus Christ, that we might be justified by the faith of Christ, and not by the works of the law: for by the works of the law shall no flesh be justified.
Galatians 2:16 (KJV)

Giving others the benefit of the doubt costs us nothing, but it can change everything. Choosing to believe the best about someone—even in the worst of circumstances—tells them they are justified until proven otherwise. Studies show that people who extend the benefit of the doubt are happier compared to those who default to blame.[1]

God gives us more than the benefit of the doubt. He gives us Jesus, and through Jesus we are truly justified. I've heard "just-i-fied" defined as "just-as-if" I've never sinned. Through Jesus we have "atonement" or "at-one-ment," restoring us to unity with God. When we are "at one" with Him, we begin to see others through His loving perspective, giving them the benefit of the doubt, just as He sees the best in us. Imagine how giving the benefit of the doubt to our spouses could change the atmosphere in our homes. Picture how holidays with family could become more joyful when we choose to believe the best in one another. Visualize the healing and unity that could flourish across our nation if we extended this same grace to fellow Americans.

How does it make you feel when someone gives you the benefit of the doubt and believes the best?

Prayer to flourish: Heavenly Father, thank You for seeing the best in me, for giving me the benefit of the doubt. But more than anything, thank You for sending Your Son to save me. I am justified (*just as if* I had never sinned) and that feels great! Amen.

---

1. https://greatergood.berkeley.edu/article/item/what_happens_when_you_give_people_the_benefit_of_the_doubt#: (accessed 6/29/24)

A Model of Kindness

I can already hear one of you agreeing by saying, "Sounds good. You take care of the faith department, I'll handle the works department." Not so fast. You can no more show me your works apart from your faith than I can show you my faith apart from my works. Faith and works, works and faith, fit together hand in glove.

James 2:18 (MSG)

Mister Rogers may not have fit the mold of a tall, dark, and handsome GQ model, but he was undeniably a model of kindness. Esquire magazine once honored him on their cover as a "New American Hero," featuring him in his signature red cardigan—a sweater lovingly knit by his mother, now displayed at the Smithsonian Institution.[1] Oscar-winning actor Tom Hanks wore this same iconic cardigan in *Won't You Be My Neighbor?*, a film that became the highest-grossing biographical documentary ever made. Those who knew Fred Rogers best shared that he cared little about wealth, living simply with his wife of 51 years. Fred believed that teaching through example was just as powerful—if not more so—than preaching. Rising every day at 4:30 a.m., he dedicated time to prayer and Bible reading, grounding himself in God's Word.[2] Fred Rogers didn't just speak about kindness; he lived it daily through small acts of generosity, compassion, and love. His life reminds us that faith in action is a powerful testimony, one that can leave an eternal legacy.

When has someone's good deed spoken more loudly than their words?

_____

_____

_____

Prayer to flourish: Jehovah Jireh, thank You for being my Provider. Your words and works fit together hand in glove. Together, Your provisions remind me I am loved. Please help me to model that same loving kindness to others. Amen.

---

1. http://www.neighborhoodarchive.com/publications/press/esquire/index.html (accessed 2/16/23)
2. Ibid

The Snow Cone Truck

> See how very much our Father loves us, for he calls us his children,
> and that is what we are!
> 1 John 3:1

As a child, the sound of the snow cone truck's bell could make an entire block erupt with excitement. My dad, with his generous heart, handed out quarters to our friends, creating cherished memories and plenty of happy faces. It's amusing how kids can hear that bell from a mile away but can't seem to hear their father's call to come home.

In a similar way, we're often deaf to our Heavenly Father's voice, while the world's messages ring loud and clear. The world tells us that we need more—more possessions, more accomplishments, more beauty—to be valuable. Even a single hour of television bombards us with commercials reminding us of what we lack.

But God's voice speaks a different truth. He reminds us that we are already precious, honored, and loved just as we are. When we tune out the noise of the world and lean into His voice, we begin to see ourselves as He does—deeply cherished and sufficient in His love.

Today, let's pause and quiet the distractions. Take a moment to listen for the Father's voice and the affirmations He speaks over us.

How might this reassurance change how you feel about yourself?

_____

_____

_____

Prayer to flourish: Abba (Daddy), I am forever grateful for Your love. Please help me to hear Your voice above the loud lies of commerce. With The Holy Spirit's help, transform me with Your love so that I can love others more simply and completely. Amen.

A Butterscotch Disk

We who have run for our very lives to God have every reason to grab the promised hope with both hands and never let go. It's an unbreakable spiritual lifeline, reaching past all appearances right to the very presence of God.
Hebrews 6:18-20a (MSG)

My little girl was choking! Her eyes were as big and as round as the butterscotch disk that was wedged in her windpipe. Frantic, I tried the Heimlich maneuver and started yelling for my husband, who ran up the basement stairs, flipped her upside down, and starting pounding on her back. I cried out to God, praying aloud in desperation.

Seconds turned into minutes, and just when we thought it was hopeless, God intervened, dislodging the disk. Alyssa could speak and her color returned. Her daddy flipped her right-side-up and hugged her limp little body tight. In a single breath that afternoon we went from hope starved to hope filled.

Today's reading reminds us that we can run to God in every circumstance. This prompts me to ask, what chokes your hope? Does a death or a diagnosis? A failing marriage or faltering finances? A wayward child or a worrisome lump? Addiction, abuse, or abandonment? None of us are immune from trials which leave us physically breathless.

What chokes your hope?
What do you hope for most?

_____

_____

_____

Prayer to flourish: Heavenly Father, thank You that we can do more than wish. You gave us a Savior and through Him You give us hope—an unbreakable spiritual lifeline that reaches past all appearances right into Your very presence. Please help me to grab onto that hope when I am hurting. Amen.

The Grand Canyon & Worry

> I'm absolutely convinced that nothing—nothing living or dead, angelic or demonic, today or tomorrow, high or low, thinkable or unthinkable—absolutely *nothing* can get between us and God's love because of the way that Jesus our Master has embraced us.
> Romans 8:39 (MSG)

The Grand Canyon is a mile deep, 277 miles long, and eighteen miles wide. It covers nearly 5,000 square miles, making it five times the size of Rhode Island.[1] It's awe inspiring to think that water from a single river carved this canyon.

In my life I have found that worry is like a river; it can carve deep canyons in my mind. We all know what it's like to fall headfirst into canyons of worry. But when we do, Jesus is there to save us from drowning in our fears.

Today's Scripture reading reminds us that deep canyons or rocky ridges will not keep God from being right there with us in our worst, worry-filled moments, offering His steady presence and peace. How do we recognize God's embrace in the midst of worry? Through love. His perfect love casts out fear, reminding us that He is our refuge and strength. Just as the Colorado River has the power to create something breathtaking, God's love has the power to transform the landscape of our lives.

What worries you most?

_____

_____

_____

Prayer to flourish: Emmanuel—You are with us. I give my worries to you. Thank You for the comforting promise of Your presence in the midst of my anxiety-producing worries. Please help me to trust You with those I hold most dear. I may not know what my future holds, but I know You hold my future. Amen.

---

1. https://www.doi.gov/blog/13-things-you-didnt-know-about-grand-canyon-national-park (accessed 10/25/22)

The Steak Sermon

Through us, he brings knowledge of Christ. Everywhere we go, people breathe in the exquisite fragrance. Because of Christ, we give off a sweet scent rising to God, which is recognized by those on the way of salvation—an aroma redolent with life.
2 Corinthians 2:14b-15a (MSG)

My husband would say there's nothing better than the savory aroma of a sizzling Kansas City Strip. I once had a pastor who grilled a steak right in front of the pulpit while he preached. It was one of the best sermons he ever delivered because it was mouth-watering and memorable.

The Bible tells us that our lives are like a sweet-smelling savor, a Christ-like fragrance rising up to God. While I've forgotten the message of many sermons, the message of the steak sermon I remember as clearly as the aroma of sizzling steaks.

When we love God and love others, we smell like Christ and bring a smile to the face of our Father. Acts of kindness make our lives more fragrant to God. Seeing our neighbors and loving them as if they were Jesus makes our lives and our world sweeter. When I leave a room, I want there to be an aroma of love that lingers.

If your life was a fragrance, how would others say you smell?

Prayer to flourish: Holy God, sometimes the things I think, say and do are foul. Please transform my stinky thoughts, words, and ways so that my life is a sweet-smelling fragrance. Please help me to be pleasing to You, bringing You glory. Amen.

Eve and Me

> If you love me, show it by doing what I've told you.
> John 14:15 (MSG)

Shopping and scrolling social media can be fun, but it's also dangerously tempting when I focus on what I don't have and start craving more. When I lose sight of my blessings and fixate on what I lack, I realize I'm not so different from Eve in the Garden of Eden.

The forbidden fruit looked good, and the promise of being wise like God sounded even better. So Eve bought into what the devil was selling. But her disobedience wasn't good—disobedience never is. Eating the forbidden fruit brought her shame, blame, and regret. It left her exposed, naked, and afraid.

God, however, wants to protect us from these bad choices. He longs for us to trust Him and follow His guidance. As today's

Scripture reminds us, our obedience is an expression of our love for Him.

Like Eve, when we give in to our desires and think God is withholding something from us, we're being deceived. Instead, let's learn from Eve's story to trust and obey the One who is truly good, rather than chasing what merely *looks* good in the moment. His plans for us are always better than anything we could crave or imagine.

When have you chosen what looked good but turned out to be bad?

_____

_____

_____

Prayer to flourish: Holy Spirit, please help me control my cravings. Help me to crave those things that truly satisfy, to be obedient and refuse those things that will bring me harm. Thank You for helping me to deny my flesh so that my spirit grows stronger each day. Amen.

I'm Not That Bad!

> Change your life, not just your clothes.
> Come back to God, *your* God.
> And here's why: God is kind and merciful.
> He takes a deep breath, puts up with a lot,
> This most patient God, extravagant in love,
> always ready to cancel catastrophe.
> Joel 2:13 (MSG)

"Well, at least I'm not that bad," I often quietly console myself. It's easy to look around and find someone whose flaws seem greater than our own. But comparing ourselves to others doesn't change the truth about our own shortcomings.

The Bible is filled with the stories of the kings of Israel and Judah—a list of what not to do. Many turned their backs on God, but King

Manasseh took sin to another level. He built altars to idols inside God's holy temple, an offense as unthinkable as inviting a second spouse into your home. He practiced witchcraft and even sacrificed his own sons to false gods. Manasseh's sins were depraved and shocking.

Yet, his story doesn't end in despair. When Manasseh repented, God forgave him and restored him to the throne. This powerful story reminds us that no one is too far gone to be saved. No matter how low we've sunk, God's extravagant love is ready to welcome us home.

Manasseh's renewal speaks to my heart, reminding me that God longs for us to return to Him. He doesn't dwell on where we've been but rejoices in our decision to come back into His embrace.

What areas of your life do you need God to renew?

_____

_____

_____

Prayer to flourish: Creator God, You make all things new and You can renew me. Please take and remake my mistakes into learnings that help me become more like Your Son. Thank You for His example and Spirit to be my inspiration for transformation. Amen.

A Thorn

> So to keep me from becoming proud, I was given a thorn
> in my flesh, a messenger from Satan
> to torment me and keep me from becoming proud.
> Three different times I begged the Lord to take it away.
> 2 Corinthians 12:7-8

A thorn in the flesh demands attention. We can each relate to pain. Sometimes it is physical pain, like splinters embedded deep under our nail bed, debilitating arthritis that holds our joints hostage, or an old injury that won't heal. Other times it's the mental pain of knowing an addiction has stolen decades of dreams from a loved one. Or maybe it's the mental strain of overwhelming debt that bankrupts hope for a home despite years of hard work. It might be the pain of an unfaithful spouse or an unmotivated child. Maybe you're not physically sick but you're worried sick and you can't shake the feeling.

Maybe it's not sickness you face, but anxiety that keeps you awake at night, pacing and praying.

Like Paul prayed three times that his painful thorn be removed, we beg God for help. While God answered Paul's prayer, it wasn't the answer he wanted. "Each time he (God) said, 'My grace is all you need. My power works best in weakness.' So now I am glad to boast about my weaknesses, so that the power of Christ can work through me."

This reminds us that while God may not remove the challenges we face, He provides exactly what we need—His sustaining grace. Our Heavenly Father sees past, present, and future and always has our best interests at heart. In His wisdom, He answers our prayers in ways that strengthen and refine us, allowing His power to shine through our weakness.

When have you felt frustrated by a "thorn"?

_____

_____

_____

Prayer to flourish: Jehovah Jireh, You are my Provider, and Your grace is sufficient for me. Help me when I am in pain, distressed, or depressed. You have my best interests at heart, and I trust You in my weakness to give me strength to endure. Amen.

First Things First

You can't worship two gods at once. Loving one god, you'll end up hating the other. Adoration of one feeds contempt for the other. You can't worship God and Money both.
Matthew 6:24 (MSG)

"Technology is a useful servant but a dangerous master."[1] It's fascinating that Nobel Peace Prize winner Dr. Christian Lange said these words back in 1921, a time when cars were just becoming part of daily life. His observation remains strikingly relevant today as technology continues to evolve and shape our lives. Modern innovations help keep us connected, but they can also blur the lines between virtual and real relationships. Too often, emojis replace genuine smiles, and scrolling through social media fills the moments once reserved for meaningful conversations. Don't get me wrong—I'm grateful for technology. It allows me to stay in touch with high school friends who live two states away and former Sunday school students who are now parents. Yet, if I'm honest, I sometimes give technology more of my time than I should—whether it's social media, funny videos, or online shopping.

Today's Scripture reminds us to keep first things first. Technology can be a powerful servant, but it should never become our master. Instead, let's ensure that God remains the center of our lives, guiding us to use these tools wisely and intentionally to deepen relationships and honor Him.

How does technology best serve you?
How does it master you?

Prayer to flourish: Lord, You alone are my Master. I serve You out of love, and I love others because You first loved me. Thank You for the gift of technology. Like every good gift, it can be abused. Please help me keep technology in its place as my servant, never letting it master me. Amen.

---

1. https://www.nobelprize.org/prizes/peace/1921/lange/lecture/ (accessed 5/14/23)

Mercy and Grace

I will go home to my father and say, "Father, I have sinned against both heaven and you, and I am no longer worthy of being called your son. Please take me on as a hired servant." But his father said to the servants, "Quick! Bring the finest robe in the house and put it on him. Get a ring for his finger and sandals for his feet. And kill the calf we have been fattening. We must celebrate with a feast, for this son of mine was dead and has now returned to life. He was lost, but now he is found." So the party began.
Luke 15:18, 22-24

Grace and mercy: both are gifts from God, but which is greater? If you could choose just one, which would it be? For me, I would always choose grace. Grace is God's idea, and it goes beyond mercy. In today's reading about the prodigal son, the father offers more than mercy. Mercy would have simply accepted the son's apology and allowed him to return home as a servant. But the father goes further—he offers grace. He dresses his son in a royal robe, places a signet ring on his finger (symbolizing access to all his wealth), and celebrates his return with a feast featuring the fatted calf.

While we each need mercy, God desires to give us so much more. He pours out His extravagant grace upon us. He throws us a celebration and welcomes us back with open arms. No matter how far we have wandered or how long we've been away, grace is there, running to greet us. Grace loves unconditionally and forgives without hesitation.

Like the father in today's parable, our Heavenly Father is always watching the horizon, eager to welcome us home. His grace is abundant, boundless, and always ready to embrace us.

When have you experienced grace?
When have you extended grace?

_____

_____

_____

Prayer to flourish: Heavenly Father, thank You for being merciful and for extending unmerited grace. I am grateful for Your audacious love for me. Teach me how to love others like You love me. Amen.

Faith and Face Transformation

> All of us! Nothing between us and God, our faces shining with the brightness of his face. And so we are transfigured much like the Messiah, our lives gradually becoming brighter and more beautiful as God enters our lives and we become like him.
> 2 Corinthians 3:18 (MSG)

God invites us to see His face so He can transform our face. Heaven knows, with each passing decade my face is transformed by gravity—my neck sags and my eyes develop bags. While I may question the promises of expensive anti-aging creams, I fully trust the promises of God.

Those who spend time with God are profoundly transformed. Paul describes this beautifully in Romans 12:2: *"Take your everyday, ordinary life—your sleeping, eating, going-to-work, and walking-*

around life—and place it before God as an offering... Fix your attention on God. You'll be changed from the inside out."

When we reflect God's glory, we radiate His light. Lifting our face to the Son brings a glow like no other. Moses' face became radiant after speaking with God. Jesus' face shone like the sun as He met with Elijah and Moses in God's presence. Even Stephen's face reflected a heavenly glow as he beheld his Savior.

More than any anti-aging gel, the most effective way to give our faces—and our hearts—a lasting glow is to spend time with God. When we seek Him, His presence transforms us, allowing His beauty to shine through our lives.

What might you remove from your schedule to spend time with your Creator?

_____

_____

_____

Prayer to flourish: Lord, I want to shine for you. Please give me an unquenchable thirst for you. Thank You for Your Teacher, The Holy Spirit, to help me become better informed and beautifully transformed by Your Word. Amen.

God Still Can

Because we are his children, God has sent the Spirit of his Son into our hearts, prompting us to call out, "Abba, Father." Now you are no longer a slave but God's own child. And since you are his child, God has made you his heir.

Galatians 4:6-7

Sometimes, I feel so overwhelmed that I'm tempted to call it quits. It's in those moments that I most need to turn to passages like today's reading. I need to remind myself that love still wins, prayer still works, Jesus still saves, and God still calls you and me His children.

The nightly news won't fill us with peace, but God still can. Buying the latest gadgets or toys won't bring lasting joy, but God still can. Securing the most impressive job title won't make us eternally rich, but God still can.

When I raid the pantry, it won't satisfy my hunger for contentment, but God still can. Filling my closet with the latest fashions won't make me timelessly irresistible, but God still can.

God finds us so irresistible that He came down to earth, taking on our sin, to make us part of His forever family. On days when we feel like giving up, we can cling to this truth: love still wins. Prayer still works. Jesus still saves. And God still calls us His beloved children.

How does it make you feel knowing you can call God your Abba (Daddy)?

Prayer to flourish: Abba Father, thank You for loving me unconditionally. While earthly fathers fail, Your love is unfailing. Thank You for making me part of Your forever family. Please help me to cry out to You first not last. To trust You first, not after all else has failed. I love You Abba and am grateful for Your perfect love despite my imperfections. Amen.

Marriage and Hybrid Cars

A man leaves his father and mother and is joined to his wife, and
the two are united into one. This is a great mystery, but it is an
illustration of the way Christ and the church are one.
So again I say, each man must love his wife as he loves himself, and
the wife must respect her husband.
Ephesians 5:31-33

Marriage has a lot in common with hybrid cars. Just as a hybrid car runs on both electricity and gas, I am fueled by love, while my husband is fueled by respect. When we communicate with love and respect, our words sound and feel different—just as hybrid cars sound and feel different from traditional ones.

During disagreements, my husband could say one thing, but I might hear something entirely different. Similarly, he often reminds me that it's not just *what* I say, but *how* I say it. If my tone comes across as disrespectful, he may not even hear my words. On the other hand, if his demeanor feels unloving, I find it hard to truly listen.

We've discovered that love and respect make our communication more effective and reduces the "harmful emissions" of misunderstandings and conflict. Much like hybrid cars are designed for efficiency, love and respect keep our marriage running more smoothly. While we still have a lot to learn, these two essentials are fueling our growth and helping us move forward together.

When your spouse, father, or mother speaks with an unloving tone, how does it make you feel? How does it effect the words you hear?

_____

_____

_____

Prayer to flourish: Christ, You are the bridegroom of the church. Please help me to always respect You and others in both my words and works. Thank You for loving me. Amen.

Wisdom Is Vertical

*If you need wisdom, ask our generous God,
and he will give it to you. He will not rebuke you for asking.*
James 1:5

I've heard it said that knowledge is horizontal, but wisdom is vertical. The Bible reminds us that knowledge will eventually pass away.[1] This truth is evident in our ever-changing world. For example, the most brilliant scientists of past generations once believed the earth was flat—an idea that is now obsolete. Knowledge evolves, and what we see as certain today may become outdated tomorrow.

As a pharmacist, I see this firsthand. Every day, new discoveries revolutionize the way we treat diseases like heart disease and cancer. Medications and procedures that were once cutting-edge are now replaced by more advanced options. While knowledge has a shelf life, wisdom endures. Wisdom transcends time and change because its foundation is in God.

In today's reading, James assures us that wisdom is a gift from God. Unlike knowledge, wisdom isn't something we can earn or acquire on our own, and it isn't guaranteed with age. Even young King Solomon, known as the wisest man in the Bible, gained his wisdom not through experience but by humbly asking God for it.

No matter your age, you can do the same. Ask for wisdom today. Ask often. God, who gives generously, is faithful to grant wisdom to those who seek Him.

What is the wisest thing you have ever done? What is the most foolish?

_____

_____

_____

Prayer to flourish: Wise Father, thank You for the gift of wisdom to discern Your will for my life. Life is full of daily decisions. Help me to be wise beyond my years in how I use my knowledge. I want to bring You glory every day of my life. Amen.

---

1. 1 Corinthians 13:8

A Spiritual Quest Through Questions

After breakfast Jesus asked Simon Peter, "Simon son of John, do you love me more than these?" "Yes, Lord," Peter replied, "you know I love you." "Then feed my lambs," Jesus told him. Jesus repeated the question: "Simon son of John, do you love me?" "Yes, Lord," Peter said, "you know I love you." "Then take care of my sheep," Jesus said. A third time he asked him, "Simon son of John, do you love me?" Peter was hurt that Jesus asked the question a third time. He said, "Lord, you know everything. You know that I love you." Jesus said, "Then feed my sheep."
John 21:15-19

My rambunctious grandson, Elijah David, asks countless questions, and I'll admit, my patience sometimes wears thin. But Jesus never grew tired of questions. During His ministry He asked over 300 of them—questions like, *"Where is your faith?" "Why are you afraid?"* and *"Do you want to get well?"* These weren't just questions for His followers of old; they remain for us today. Jesus, in His omniscience, doesn't ask questions to gain knowledge. Instead, He asks to invite reflection, spark investigation, and lead to transformation. Among His most profound questions was the one He asked Simon Peter three times: *"Do you love me?"* Each repetition deepened Peter's self-awareness and solidified his calling to care for others.

Jesus' questions are invitations to journey deeper in faith. Out of over 300 recorded questions, He directly answered only three. His purpose wasn't to provide easy answers but to ignite a lifelong pursuit of knowing Him more fully. Today, as we hear His questions, may we find not just answers, but the transformation He desires for us.

What questions do you have for Jesus that might result in spiritual quests?

_____

_____

_____

Prayer to flourish: Lord Jesus, thank You that You welcome my questions. More than literacy in Your Word, help me to experience intimacy through Your Word. Help me to trust Your answers, especially when they are hard to understand or accept. Amen.

Chill Out and Lemon Down

> Be still, and know that I am God!
> Psalm 46:10

Chillax. Chill Out. Lemon Down. And Moss—these are all expressions that communicate the same idea: slow down and relax. Chill and relax combine to form the word "chillax" (which I recently learned is called a portmanteau). "Lemon Down" paints a vivid image of someone cooling off poolside with a tall glass of lemonade. But moss? That's a new one for me. Could it be because moss grows slowly in cool, undisturbed places?

Eugene Peterson paraphrases today's Scripture beautifully, saying, *"Step out of the traffic! Take a long, loving look at me, your High God, above politics, above everything."* Is God telling us to "lemon down" and chillax when He says, "Be still"? I believe He is—but it goes deeper than that. In Hebrew, "be still" is *raphah*, meaning to loosen your grip.[1] And "know" is *yada*, meaning to personally experience.[2] So, when God says, *"Be still and know,"* He's not asking us to do nothing in moments of anxiety. He's calling us to release our hold on what is temporary, so we can grasp tightly onto Him, the eternal. When life feels overwhelming, let's loosen our grip on fleeting concerns and hold firmly to the peace of knowing God.

How might God be calling you to "be still and know" He is God today?

_____

_____

_____

Prayer to flourish: Abba Father, some days can feel like a rat race. My work week can leave me ragged. My housework is never done. My responsibilities are never-ending. In the midst of the chaos of life, please help me to be still, to relax my grip on temporal things so that I can rest, knowing You hold me eternally. Thank You for being my Father. Amen.

---

1. https://biblehub.com/hebrew/7503.htm NAS Exhaustive Concordance NASB Translation (accessed 5/8/23)
2. https://www.biblehub.com/hebrew/3045.htm (accessed 05/05/23)

Be A Star

> "You are the light of the world—like a city on a hilltop that cannot be hidden. No one lights a lamp and then puts it under a basket. Instead, a lamp is placed on a stand, where it gives light to everyone in the house. In the same way, let your good deeds shine out for all to see, so that everyone will praise your heavenly Father.
> Matthew 5:14-16

Martin Luther King Jr. once said, *"Darkness cannot drive out darkness; only light can do that. Hate cannot drive out hate; only love can do that."*[1] These words, as powerful today as when they were first spoken, remind us that the forces of love and light are the only true antidotes to the darkness and hatred we encounter in the world. Dr. King's message aligns with today's Scripture reading. In his final speech, Dr. King offered another profound truth: *"Only when it's dark enough can you see the stars."*[2] His words paint a vivid picture of hope. In the darkest times, even the smallest light can shine brilliantly. Together, we have the privilege and responsibility to illuminate a world in need, just as stars brighten the night sky. Every act of kindness, each gesture of grace, becomes a radiant beacon that points back to God's glory. Opportunities to shine are everywhere. A thoughtful word, a helping hand, or even just listening with compassion can make a difference. God calls us to reflect His love and be a source of hope for those around us. Your light is needed—perhaps now more than ever.

How might you shine today, making your corner of the world a brighter place?

_____

_____

_____

Prayer to flourish: Jesus, You are the Light of the World. As a Christian (or little Christ) I want to highlight Your love by how I love others. Thank You for Your unconditional love. In a world that is divided and dark, help me bring peace and light through kindness. Amen.

---

1. https://www.nps.gov/mlkm/learn/quotations.htm (accessed 7/7/22)
2. https://www.goodnewsnetwork.org/martin-luther-king-jr-quote-about-stars/ (accessed 5/9/23)

Hindsight and Foresight

He comforts us in all our troubles so that we can comfort others.
When they are troubled, we will be able to give them
the same comfort God has given us.
2 Corinthians 1:4

In my twenties, living two states away from my mother, as a first-time mom of a toddler who didn't speak until she was nearly three, I was worried sick. I worked with her daily on her diction, fearing her speech development was lagging. Then one day, the truth came out. While with her Godmother, as someone commented on her quiet nature, my daughter spoke up as clear as a bell, retorting, "I CAN TALK IF I WANT TO!" Apparently, she just hadn't "wanted to" before—pointing and grunting had been enough to get her needs met.

Looking back now, I can see those worries in a different light. At the time, though, I couldn't help but compare her development to other children her age, feeling unsure. Now, as I watch my daughter experience similar concerns with her son—an only child who also communicates with grunts and gestures—I can empathize deeply.

Today's Scripture reminds us that each of us is uniquely equipped for ministry. As moms and grandmas, our hindsight can become another's foresight. The trials we've endured give us the wisdom to comfort and guide others. Our greatest pain can become our greatest purpose. When we comfort others, we find comfort ourselves. Blessings given often return to us—like a boomerang of grace.

What trial has become a triumph?
How might you help someone be triumphant too?

_____

_____

_____

Prayer to flourish: Precious Savior, You saved me. The trial of the cross became our triumph of salvation. Thank You for suffering for me. Please help me serve others who are suffering through both small and large trials, to come alongside them so they can experience relief and triumphant victory. Amen.

Features That Frustrate

The commandments of the Lord are right, bringing joy to the heart. The commands of the Lord are clear, giving insight for living.
Psalm 19:8

With all its automated features, my car sometimes frustrates me. For instance, it refuses to let me lock the door if my key fob is accidentally left inside. While this feature saves me from locking myself out, I find it inexplicably annoying. Dashboard lights flash if I change lanes without signaling, and my car automatically brakes when someone unexpectedly cuts me off. On the highway, it even slows down to maintain a safe following distance.

Though I know these features are designed for my safety and the safety of others, I often feel more aggravated than appreciative. Is it because I dislike change? Do I resist being corrected? Or is it simply my tendency to push back against technology? It's probably a mix of all three.

But as I reflect, I realize these safety features are much like The Ten Commandments. They are created with my protection in mind. God's laws are designed for my best interests and those of my neighbor. They are not there to restrict me but to guide me into a life of peace, safety, and harmony.

God, our Creator, knows what will keep us safe. Just as I'm learning to trust my car's features, I am reminded to trust His guidance even more.

Have you ever found God's commands frustrating?

_____

_____

_____

Prayer to flourish: Father, sometimes I resist Your instruction. I'm sorry for my bad attitude. Please help me align my will with Your Will. I trust You have my best interests at heart even though I may not see the full picture on this side of eternity. I love you. Amen.

On The Tough Days

Elijah was afraid and fled for his life...Alone into the wilderness...he sat down under a solitary broom tree and prayed that he might die. "I have had enough, Lord," he said. "Take my life"...Then he lay down and slept under the broom tree. But as he was sleeping, an angel touched him and told him, "Get up and eat!" He looked around and there beside his head was some bread baked on hot stones and a jar of water!

1 Kings 19:3a-6a

Some days are undeniably tough. Today's reading recounts one of those moments for the prophet Elijah. In his despair, Elijah cried out, *"Lord, I want to die."* Yet, God didn't leave him in his anguish. Instead, He sent an angel to strengthen Elijah and give him the will to live.

Growing up reading the King James Bible, I always loved how it said the angel brought Elijah cake. While bread is good, there's just something about cake—especially angel food cake—that seems to make bad days a little better! Throughout Scripture, we see God meeting people in their moments of need.

Sometimes, He sends angels to deliver heavenly nourishment. But more often, He chooses ordinary people like you and me to deliver His extraordinary love. Today's Scripture reminds us that love can be expressed in simple, tangible ways. Sharing food not only nourishes the body but also expresses kindness that nourishes the soul. When we reach out in love, we become light-bearers, reflecting God's love and easing the heavy burdens of those around us. Every small act of kindness, like offering a meal, becomes a beacon of hope in someone's life. God's love is at work through us.

When have you experienced angelic kindness?

Prayer to flourish: Savior, I'm far from angelic, but might You use me to deliver kindness to someone in need? I have ordinary skills but know that You can use these everyday skills to help those praying for an angelic miracle. Thank You for allowing me to impact eternity. Amen.

Better not Bitter

> Don't you see, you planned evil against me
> but God used those same plans for my good.
> Genesis 50:20 (MSG)

Being favored feels incredible, but being forgotten can feel unbearable. Today's verses were spoken by Joseph to his eleven brothers—the same brothers who betrayed him and sold him into slavery. They were jealous because Joseph was their father's favorite son, a fact made even more obvious by the gift of a special, colorful coat.

We've all had moments when we've felt betrayed and forgotten. Perhaps at home, in relationships with a spouse or siblings, or at work, dealing with colleagues or bosses. These moments are humbling, and if we're honest, they hurt.

But Joseph's story reminds us of this profound truth: good can come from bad. What others intend for harm, God can use for good. When I repeat Joseph's words out loud, *"You meant it to harm me, but God used it for good,"* they help heal my heart and shift my focus to the good that may be just over the horizon.

Joseph didn't let bitterness take root. Instead, he chose to grow better, becoming more refined in his faith. He relied on God in both the bad years and the good ones. Just as Joseph found favor, we can too. God promises to bring good even from what others meant to harm us.

When has someone done something to hurt you? Has God brought any good from it yet?

_____

_____

_____

Prayer to flourish: Abba Father, you tell me to bring all the bad I have experienced to You so that You can wring every drop from the experience and bring good from it. Thank You that You are trustworthy even when I don't immediately see the good. Please help me to forgive those who have intentionally and unintentionally hurt me. Please take my bitterness and make me better. Amen.

Fatigued or Flourishing?

Your kingdom come,
your will be done, on earth as it is in heaven.
Matthew 6:10

In just five verses, Jesus taught us how to pray through The Lord's Prayer. Today's reading focuses on the second verse: "Your kingdom come, your will be done, on earth as it is in heaven." These words remind us of the need to align our lives with God's Will. Jesus knew that for His kingdom to come and for our lives, as well as the lives of those around us, to truly flourish, we must surrender our own plans and trust in His divine purpose.

It's tempting to rely on our own willpower, striving to control every outcome. Yet this constant effort can leave us drained and discouraged. God never intended for us to live that way. Instead, He calls us to rest in Him, to hand over our worries, and to trust that His ways are higher than ours. When we surrender to His Will, we find renewed strength, peace, and the ability to flourish.

Choosing God's Will over our own is an act of faith—a daily decision to trust His wisdom and His timing. As we live in obedience, we catch glimpses of His kingdom here on earth, a reflection of His perfect Will in heaven.

What part of your life would flourish if you surrendered fully to God's Will today?

___

___

___

Prayer to flourish: Lord, I surrender my will to You. Align my heart with Yours and guide me to trust Your plans. May Your kingdom come and Your Will be done in my life today and always. Thank You for Your faithfulness and unending grace. In Jesus' name, Amen.

Velcro® and My Heart

> Make allowance for each other's faults, and forgive anyone who
> offends you. Remember, the Lord forgave you,
> so you must forgive others.
> Colossians 3:13

Late one night, I received a hurtful text from a friend. Not wanting to dwell on her words, I deleted it, knowing that if I didn't, I'd reread it over and over. Yet, though the text was gone, the sting lingered. My heart felt like Velcro®, with her critical words firmly stuck to its surface.

Sometimes, friendships can be sticky. Just as Velcro® clings to threads, our hearts often cling to offenses. So how do we get unstuck? How do we forgive—and can we really forget?

Oddly enough, the first step to forgetting might actually be remembering. When I reflect on how God forgives my harsh words, my mistakes, and my countless shortcomings, I'm reminded to extend the same mercy to others. Every time I pray The Lord's Prayer, I reaffirm this truth: "Forgive us our trespasses, as we forgive those who trespass against us."

I want God to forget my flaws and failures. Thankfully, He promises to do just that. Isaiah 43:25 tells us that He blots out our sins and remembers them no more. Letting go of hurt is far from natural—it's supernatural. It requires The Holy Spirit's help to release the grip of pain and allow healing to begin.

While we may always remember the fact of the offense, God can help us let go of the emotional weight it carries. Just as a mother remembers the details of her child's birth but forgets the pain, we can trust The Holy Spirit to help us focus on the good and heal the hurt. Velcro® holds on. But God empowers us to let go.

When and with whom have you wanted to have an offense forgiven and forgotten?

_____

_____

_____

Prayer to flourish: Merciful Jesus, thank You for sending your Holy Spirit, my Comforter, to help me forgive when I am hurt. While I may remember the event, please help me forget the pain. Amen.

Roy G. Biv and White Light

Jesus spoke to the people once more and said, "I am the light of the world. If you follow me, you won't have to walk in darkness, because you will have the light that leads to life.
John 8:12

Remember Roy G. Biv? This playful acronym helps us recall the vibrant colors of a rainbow. I still remember the amazement I felt in sixth grade science class when I learned that white light contains all the colors of the rainbow. It seemed impossible, but a crystal prism proved otherwise—separating the colors and allowing each wavelength to shine. Without the prism, the wavelengths cancel each other, and the light appears white.

This reminds me of God's grace. Just as white light cancels the individuality of each color, God's grace cancels our individual sins, no matter how "colorful" or varied they are. Through Christ, we are made pure, as radiant as white light.

Light is powerful. It illuminates, comforts, and warms like sunshine warming our skin, God's love warms and renews our spirits. In today's reading Jesus proclaimed, "I am the light of the world. Whoever follows me will never walk in darkness but will have the light of life." His light dispels darkness, guiding and transforming us.

Like a prism reveals the beauty within white light, God's love reveals our true, forgiven selves. Let's embrace His grace, shine brightly, and reflect His love to the world.

When you imagine grace, what color comes to mind? How is Jesus asking you to follow Him today?

_____

_____

_____

Prayer to flourish: Jesus, thank You for extending Your gift of grace to me. I've done nothing to earn Your grace. I can do nothing to lose Your grace. Your grace is not based on how good I am. It is based on how good You are. Please help me shine for you. Amen.

Spaghetti at the Airport

> Meanwhile, the moment we get tired in the waiting, God's Spirit is right alongside helping us along. If we don't know how or what to pray, it doesn't matter. He does our praying in and for us, making prayer out of our wordless sighs, our aching groans. He knows us far better than we know ourselves, knows our pregnant condition, and keeps us present before God.
>
> Romans 8:26-27 (MSG)

My dad once interrupted my husband at work with an urgent message: "Meet me at the airport for spaghetti in one hour." Since my dad struggled with dementia, the message made perfect sense to him, but it left my husband completely befuddled. My parents lived seven hours away from the Kansas City airport, in the small farming community of Mattoon, Illinois. Knowing Dad had occasionally managed to slip away from my mom's watchful eye in the past, my husband grew concerned. He quickly texted me, "Your dad needs you to pick him up at the airport, and he's hungry for spaghetti."

Confused, I called my parents. My mom answered, and together we unraveled Dad's message. We realized Dad had accidentally called my husband, Dave, instead of their neighbor, also named Dave. My parents and their neighbor were planning to meet at the tiny Mattoon airport restaurant, known for its spaghetti special, that day.

Relieved, I laughed. This situation reminded me of a comforting truth: even when others don't understand us, God does. When we are too weary or discouraged to put our needs into words, The Holy Spirit intercedes. Today's Scripture assures us that He gives meaning to our "wordless sighs and aching groans."

When do you find praying most difficult?

_____

_____

_____

Prayer to flourish: My Savior, thank You for sending me Your best—Your Holy Spirit—when I am at my worst. When I am exhausted and confused, Your Spirit intercedes for me. While others may not understand me, You do. I love You, Lord. Amen.

Mud, Spit and the Right Question

> As Jesus was walking along, he saw a man who had been blind from birth. "Rabbi," his disciples asked him, "why was this man born blind? Was it because of his own sins or his parents' sins?" "It was not because of his sins or his parents' sins," Jesus answered. "This happened so the power of God could be seen."
>
> John 9:1-3

Lately, bad news has come like tsunami waves and I'm exhausted. When bad things happen, I often find myself crying out, "Why?" In today's reading, Jesus' disciples asked a similar question—"Why was this man born blind?" Jesus gently corrected them: "You're asking the wrong question. You're looking for someone to blame. Look instead for what God can do."

It's so easy to fall into the trap of the blame game. Trusting God during a trial is far harder. Yet, I'm learning to ask better questions:

"How can this bad situation showcase God's goodness? Can this bring Him glory?" This shift in perspective changes everything. Instead of spiraling into depression, I begin to look for hidden treasures of grace buried within the struggle. Through eyes of faith, I can see God at work, even in the darkest moments.

What the world labels as "bad," God can use for incredible good. Some might see mud and spit as messy and unclean, but in the hands of our Savior, mud and spit healed a blind man's eyes. If God can use something so ordinary to do the extraordinary, surely He can transform the trials in my life too. With Him, all things are possible.

What bad thing in your life might Jesus be able to use to bring good to you?

_____

_____

_____

Prayer to flourish: Lord Jesus, I don't like mud or spit in my eyes. I don't like to be corrected or criticized. I dislike waiting and conceding. I hate to be sick. And I despise being hurt. Yet all these bad things You can use for my ultimate benefit. Please help me to trust you. I know you're faithful and trustworthy. Amen.

Time to Stand or to Kneel

So, what do you think? With God on our side like this, how can we lose? If God didn't hesitate to put everything on the line for us, embracing our condition and exposing himself to the worst by sending his own Son, is there anything else he wouldn't gladly and freely do for us? And who would dare tangle with God by messing with one of God's chosen?
Romans 8:31-33 (MSG)

When life gives you more than you can stand, it may be time to kneel. Kneeling in prayer gives us the strength to stand again. Today's reading poses a timeless question: "If God is for us, who can be against us?" This question is more than a reflection—it's a battle cry, one I hold tightly to when it feels like the world is against me.

On days when the weight of life seems unbearable, I find comfort in today's Scripture. This chapter overflows with hope, culminating in a powerful promise: "Nothing can ever separate us from Christ's love. Does it mean God no longer loves us if we have trouble or calamity, or are persecuted, or hungry, or destitute, or in danger, or threatened with death? No, despite all these things, overwhelming victory is ours through Christ, who loves us."

Life's challenges might knock us down, but they can't keep us there. When we kneel in prayer, we rise with renewed strength, knowing that God is for us. His love is unshakable, constant, and victorious. No trial or trouble can separate us from His care. In every battle, we can trust that God has our back.

When do you feel most defeated?

———————————————————————

———————————————————————

———————————————————————

Prayer to flourish: Almighty Father, some days I feel like the world is against me, but the fact is that You are on my side. Feelings are fickle. Facts are firm. I stand on Your promises. I kneel in expectant hope. Thank You for Your trustworthy commitment to be with me always. Amen.

J.O.Y.

> Be generous with the different things God gave you, passing them around so all get in on it: if words, let it be God's words; if help, let it be God's hearty help. That way, God's bright presence will be evident in everything through Jesus, and he'll get all the credit as the One mighty in everything—encores to the end of time.
> 1 Peter 4:10-11 (MSG)

Jesus wants us to be joyful! The Bible contains more than 2,700 verses about joy, happiness, gladness, pleasure, celebration, cheer, laughter, delight, jubilation, feasting, merriment, blessing, and exultation.[1] Yet in a world flooded with sorrow, keeping our joy afloat can feel like an impossible task. Recently, I heard an acronym for JOY that's rooted in Scripture: "J" for Jesus, "O" for others, and "Y" for yourself.

This simple yet profound acronym only works when I put Jesus first. Resting in Him renews my strength and readies me to serve others with my God-given gifts. But when I reverse the order—putting others before Jesus—I quickly grow weary. Without being filled by Him, my joy boat starts to sink. Tears of frustration inevitably follow, leaving me waterlogged and worn thin. Jesus reminds us that true joy is found in Him. When I take time to be filled with His Word, rest in His presence, spend time in creation, and connect with other believers, I find the strength to serve joyfully. While life may test our limits, joy becomes unsinkable when Jesus is at the helm.

When have you experienced Biblical joy recently?

_____

_____

_____

Prayer to flourish: Lord, the world says, "Look out for #1." Please grant me wisdom to discern when I should give and when I should accept help. Thank You for the small joys you bless me with daily. Continue to open my eyes and my heart to experiencing You, the Source of all joy. Amen.

---

1. https://www.biblegateway.com/blog/2019/09/how-happiness-happens-an-interview-with-max-lucado/ (accessed 8/12/22)

Hula Hoops and Arguments

When someone gives you a hard time, respond with the supple moves of prayer, for then you are working out of your true selves, your God-created selves. This is what God does. He gives his best—the sun to warm and the rain to nourish—to everyone, regardless: the good and bad, the nice and nasty.

Matthew 5:44-47 (MSG)

Do you remember playing with hula hoops as a kid? Twirling them round and round, we shifted our weight, rocking back and forth to keep the hoop circling our waist. Interestingly, hula hoops date back to 500 BC,[1] making them even older than Jesus. Funny enough, I no longer enjoy the challenge of hula hoops like I did in my childhood. Similarly, I've lost my enthusiasm for going round and round in arguments, debating back and forth. Many of us crave being right and having the last word, but sometimes the wisest choice is to let the "hula hoop" of an argument drop to our feet. Ceasing the back-and-forth can prevent unnecessary tension. Some conversations require us to lean into the wisdom of walking away instead of engaging further.

Today's reading encourages us to respond with the gentleness of prayer instead of falling into quarrels. Choosing prayer over conflict allows us to move forward peacefully. When disagreements arise, let's trust in God's wisdom and gracefully set aside arguments that spin us in circles.

What recent argument might have ended differently if you had responded with the supple moves of prayer?

_____

_____

_____

Prayer to flourish: Lord Jesus, it feels good to get the last word. While this makes me feel like I have won the battle, I may have lost the war. Please grant me wisdom in choosing my words. Thank You for helping me control my tongue. Amen.

---

1. https://hoopnotica.com/blogs/stay-in-the-hoop/the-history-of-hula-hoops (accessed 7/7/22)

Poke Holes or Holy Work

> She is clothed with strength and dignity,
> and she laughs without fear of the future.
> Proverbs 31:25

When my son was a toddler, he loved using tools just like his daddy. Garrett always wanted to help. Once, while I was covered in paste wallpapering the living room, Garrett grabbed the screwdriver I had used to remove the outlet covers. He straddled the doorway between the living room and kitchen, rocking back and forth as he sang, "Poke holes. Poke holes. Poke holes."

It wasn't until I walked into the kitchen that I realized he was putting those words into action—poking holes in my brand-new kitchen wallpaper. While I was improving the living room wall, he was undoing the progress in the kitchen. I wanted to collapse right there on the hard tile floor and cry.

Some days, the faster I run, the less I get done. The longer I work on my to-do list, the longer it becomes. When progress feels impossible, I need encouragement. When I'm disheartened and weary, I need strength.

In those moments, I'm reminded that raising children is holy work. Today's reading reminds us that as women of faith, we are clothed with strength and dignity, and we can laugh without fear of the future. Even when life feels overwhelming, God equips us for the journey.

When have you felt like crying or giving up before a project is completed?

_____

_____

_____

Prayer to flourish: Heavenly Father, when I'm at my worst and ready to give up, prop me up. Please turn my tears into laughter. Transform my exhaustion into elation. Give me heavenly perspective on earthly problems. Thank You for my children, my husband, my health, and my home. Amen.

Loud Thoughts

> The thief's purpose is to steal and kill and destroy.
> John 10:10a

Sometimes our thoughts are so loud, they seem to shout even when unspoken. They can leave us whirring like our washer's spin cycle, clinging to the edges, spun dry and worn out.

We have an adversary who thrives on whispering lies designed to shake our "God-fidence"—our confidence in God. In today's reading, Jesus calls him what he is: a thief. This thief's purpose is to steal, kill, and destroy. His tactics are nothing new. He whispered to Eve in the garden, planting seeds of doubt, and he still whispers to us today.

But here's an important truth: while the devil may influence our thinking, he cannot read our thoughts. Only God is omniscient (all-knowing), omnipotent (all-powerful), and omnipresent (always present).[1] Satan is not. He only knows our thoughts if we give them a voice. That's why it's crucial to speak words of faith and truth aloud.

Jesus came to give us abundant life—more God-fidence, more joy, more peace. When we stand in faith, we deny the lies of the thief. Together, we can silence his whispers and embrace the abundant life Jesus promises.

When are you most challenged by loud thoughts?

___

___

___

Prayer to flourish: Almighty God, thank You for giving me joy that imparts strength. I need this when I feel washed up and spun dry. Thank You for sending Your Son so that I can experience abundant life. I am so grateful for His Spirit, The Holy Spirit, who lives within me and can comfort me, quieting my loud thoughts. Amen.

___

1. Psalm 139:23-24

Stressed and Blessed

Summing it all up, friends, I'd say you'll do best by filling your minds and meditating on things true, noble, reputable, authentic, compelling, gracious—the best, not the worst; the beautiful, not the ugly; things to praise, not things to curse. Put into practice what you learned from me, what you heard and saw and realized. Do that, and God, who makes everything work together, will work you into his most excellent harmonies.
Philippians 4:8-9 (MSG)

When I fix my thoughts on God, He faithfully fixes my flawed thoughts. Recently, I read this simple yet profound reminder: "Stop focusing on how STRESSED you are and remember how BLESSED you are!" While we don't know who first said this, one thing is certain—it's easier said than done. Stress has a way of making even simple tasks feel overwhelming.

In this particularly stressful season of my life, filled with countless changes, I've had to remind myself that it's okay to ask for help. I've learned to extend grace to myself and allow space to rest. One way I renew my spirit is by spending time outdoors, seeking God's presence in creation. When I pause to notice the subtle sights and sounds of nature, my soul finds refreshment. My focus shifts from worries to worship.

I've also found encouragement in Christian music that proclaims God's promises, as well as in the support of friends and mentors who remind me of His faithfulness. Most importantly, God's living Word redirects my thoughts. My mind's eye acts like a magnifying glass—when I focus on my blessings, my worries diminish. When I fix my thoughts on Him, He realigns my perspective, restores my peace, and faithfully fixes my thoughts.

How do you need your thoughts "fixed" today?

_____

_____

_____

Prayer to flourish: Lord, it's hard to fix my thoughts on You when the world is so loud and distracting. Please help me learn to quiet my heart by inviting Your Holy Spirit into every moment of my day. Thank You for Your peaceful harmonies amid the cacophony and chaos of life. Amen.

Friends and Shoes

So, chosen by God for this new life of love, dress in the wardrobe God picked out for you: compassion, kindness, humility, quiet strength, discipline. Be even-tempered, content with second place, quick to forgive an offense. Forgive as quickly and completely as the Master forgave you. And regardless of what else you put on, wear love. It's your basic, all-purpose garment. Never be without it.
Colossians 3:12-14 (MSG)

I've heard it said that friends and shoes have a lot in common. Good ones are hard to find, but once you do, you don't want to walk a day without them. In my opinion you can never have too many shoes or too many friends, which leads me to wonder: What type of shoe would best describe the type of friend I am to others?

I want to be a friend who is like a comfy tennis shoe, always ready to walk by their side through the hills and the valleys. Maybe you want to be like a warm boot, easy to slip into even on the coldest days. One thing is for sure. I don't want my friendship to be like a stiletto that looks good but makes life difficult and brings pain.

In today's reading Paul encourages us to wear comfy things like tenderhearted mercy, kindness, humility, gentleness, and patience. These describe someone I would want as a friend. Good friends with these comfy qualities have much in common with good shoes. Both are hard to find.

What type of shoe best describes you?

_____

_____

_____

Prayer to flourish: Lord, thank You for being my friend. Please help me to be a good friend to others. I trust you to bring Christian friends into my life to walk beside me providing wisdom and comfort. Faithful friends are gifts. You enrich my life through these friendships. Amen.

Brownies and Life

Get rid of all bitterness, rage, anger, harsh words, and slander, as well as all types of evil behavior. Instead, be kind to each other, tenderhearted, forgiving one another, just as God through Christ has forgiven you.
Ephesians 4:31-32

I'm not a pastry chef, but I do love to bake—and I'm especially known for my scrumdiddlyumptious brownies. My secret? Don't overbake them. Just one minute too long can make all the difference because brownies keep baking after they leave the oven until they cool below 150 degrees. I've learned this lesson the hard way, having baked plenty of rock-hard brownies in my day!

Brownies have a lot in common with life. I've realized that overthinking things is like overbaking brownies—it makes everything harder. Dwelling on and rehashing hurts can harden our hearts, making it even tougher to forgive.

But here's the truth: as hard as forgiving may be, holding onto hurt is even harder. Perhaps that's why today's Bible passage encourages us to be tenderhearted and gentle with one another, forgiving as quickly and thoroughly as God forgives us (Ephesians 4:32).

Soft, perfectly-baked brownies are a joy to eat, just as a softened heart brings joy to life. When we release the hurts that threaten to harden us, we create space for God's love and grace to flow. Life, like a brownie, is far sweeter when we remain tenderhearted toward others.

What hurts make your heart hard?
Who might you need to forgive to make your life more scrumptious like soft brownies?

_____

_____

_____

Prayer to flourish: Christ, You were hurt beyond comprehension when You were nailed to the cross, yet You forgave Your offenders. Please help me to keep a soft heart so that my life is sweeter both for me and those around me. Amen.

I Am Who I Am

> But Moses protested, "If I go to the people of Israel...they will ask me, 'What is his name?' God replied to Moses, "I am who I am. Say this to the people of Israel: Yahweh, the God of your ancestors—the God of Abraham, the God of Isaac, and the God of Jacob—has sent me to you. This is my eternal name, my name to remember for all generations.
> Exodus 3:13-14

For years I struggled with God's response in today's passage. "What kind of name is 'I am who I am?'" It seemed so vague. When someone asks who I am, I'm direct: "My name is Lisa Wilt." At a school event I add, "I'm Garrett and Alyssa's mom." At a social event I might say, "I'm Dave's wife." At work I share my title.

In today's reading, God does something similar; He offers more detail in the latter half of the passage: "I am Yahweh, the God of your ancestors—the God of Abraham, the God of Isaac, and the God of Jacob." But God didn't stop there. He wanted us to know Him even more personally, so He sent His Son. Jesus makes the divine tangible—Someone I can wrap my mind and heart around.

After all these years, I've come to appreciate what my English teachers might've marked as "incorrect" in this passage. God uses the present tense. He doesn't say, "I was the God of Abraham." In Revelation, He declares, "I am the Alpha and the Omega, the Beginning and the End." He is present in our past and future. And that's the profound lesson I still strive to grasp: I am a child of the great I AM. The great I AM is wherever I am.

What is your favorite name for God?

_____

_____

_____

Prayer to flourish: Yahweh, thank You for being present with me wherever I am. Help me to keep You present in my heart wherever I am. I am grateful that I am Your child. Amen.

Beautifully Broken

> Jesus took the five loaves and two fish, looked up toward heaven, and blessed them. Then, breaking the loaves into pieces, he kept giving the bread to the disciples so they could distribute it to the people. He also divided the fish for everyone to share.
> Mark 6:41

Elizabeth Elliott famously said, "If your life is broken, it may be because the pieces will feed a multitude."[1] In my early twenties, I often felt broken. As a new pharmacist, I worried about making dispensing errors and failing my patients. At home, I struggled as a wife and mother, raising my voice more than I'd like. I felt overwhelmed, inadequate, and most of all, broken. No one likes to feel broken. Brokenness brings pain—whether it's broken dreams, broken homes, or broken lives. Yet, when we feel broken, the best place to be is in our Savior's hands. He longs to take our broken pieces and make us both whole and holy. Jesus showed us the beauty of brokenness when He fed the 5,000. Taking one small boy's bread, He blessed and broke it, and that broken bread miraculously fed 5,000 men and their families. There were even twelve baskets of leftovers, a symbol that God's provision is always more than enough.

Today's reading reminds us that in Jesus' hands, what feels broken can lead to beautiful abundance. What we see as "not enough" becomes "more than enough." God can use our greatest pain to bring about our greatest purpose.

When have your painful experiences allowed you to have empathy and help others?

_____

_____

_____

Prayer to flourish: Lord, while I don't like pain and don't want to feel broken, I know that both are a part of this life. Thank You for not only comforting me in my pain but also for promising that You will use my pain for a greater purpose. Amen.

---

1. https://www.quoteambition.com/elisabeth-elliot-quotes/(accessed 10/25/22)

Need Rest?

> Then Jesus said, "Come to me, all of you who are weary and carry heavy burdens, and I will give you rest."
> Matthew 11:28

Some people seem to have it all together. They look polished and perfect, as if their lives are free of flaws. When I look at myself, I feel the opposite. I see my imperfections and sometimes feel like I'm falling apart.

But then I remember—Jesus didn't say, "Come to me, all you who have everything under control." Today's reading reminds us that Jesus invites us to come as we are, no matter how messy, flawed, or burdened we feel. He welcomes our hard-to-handle hurts, hang-ups, and habits.

Jesus calls us to walk beside Him, to partner with Him, and to learn His unforced rhythms of grace. In His company, we discover how to live freely and lightly. He doesn't require perfection—He offers rest.

When we pause and steal time away with Him, we find relief from striving and rediscover what truly matters. Jesus reminds us that even with our blemishes and brokenness, we are perfectly loved by Abba, our heavenly Daddy.

The next time you feel like you're falling short, remember this truth: You don't need to have it all together to come to Jesus. He loves you just as you are.

In what areas do you most need to learn His unforced rhythms of grace?

_____

_____

_____

Prayer to flourish: Abba Father, I need rest when my hope is worn thin and my heart is worn out. I need physical rest and spiritual rest for my soul. Thank You for providing both. I'm so grateful You welcome me when I need help carrying heavy burdens. I accept Your invitation this very moment. Amen.

The Rearview Mirror

We continue to shout our praise even when we're hemmed in with troubles, because we know how troubles can develop passionate patience in us, and how that patience in turn forges the tempered steel of virtue, keeping us alert for whatever God will do next. In alert expectancy such as this, we're never left feeling shortchanged. Quite the contrary—we can't round up enough containers to hold everything God generously
pours into our lives through The Holy Spirit!
Romans 5:3-5 (MSG)

John Maxwell writes, "Adversity is a crossroads that makes a person choose one of two paths: character or compromise. Every time people choose character, they become stronger, even if that choice brings negative consequences."[1] Centuries before Maxwell, Paul expressed this truth more profoundly in today's Scripture reading. If I'm honest, I prefer adversity when it's in my rearview mirror. It's easier to appreciate its lessons after the storm has passed. But verses like these give me strength when I'm in the thick of suffering. They remind me that God is using the challenges I face to cultivate perseverance, shape my character, and ultimately fill me with hope. Adversity may not be something we seek, but it's a powerful tool in God's hands. When we lean into Him during hard times, we emerge stronger in Christ, equipped with deeper character and unshakable hope. If you're facing a crossroads of adversity today, know that choosing to persevere with God will lead to a path of growth and transformation.

When has perseverance in your life led to good?

_____

_____

_____

Prayer to flourish: God, You are Almighty. In God we trust. As American Christians, please help us to work together as one nation, under God, indivisible, with liberty and justice for all. Help us to turn to You so that we emerge from every crisis with *the tempered steel of virtue*. Amen.

---

1. https://quotefancy.com/quote/841641/John-C-Maxwell-Adversity-is-a-crossroads-that-makes-a-person-choose-one-of-two-paths(accessed 10/23/22)

Gold, Frankincense, and Myrrh

They entered the house and saw the child with his mother, Mary, and they bowed down and worshiped him. Then they opened their treasure chests and gave him gifts of gold, frankincense, and myrrh.
Matthew 2:11

Gold, frankincense, and myrrh immediately take me to my favorite season—Christmas—no matter the time of year. These precious gifts were brought to honor Jesus, but were there really three wise men? In today's Scripture, Matthew—who worked with numbers—doesn't specify the number of visitors when he describes their gifts. The tradition of three wise men likely stems from the three gifts. Christian tradition even provides names: Casper, Melchior, and Balthasar. These gifts carried profound symbolism. Gold honored Jesus as King. Frankincense, often used in worship, acknowledged Him as God. Myrrh, a burial spice, foreshadowed His sacrificial death—His ultimate gift to humanity.[1] These scholars traveled great distances, demonstrating extraordinary devotion. Their actions challenge me to reflect on the gifts I bring to honor Jesus. While I don't have gold, frankincense, or myrrh, I've been entrusted with time, talents, and treasures. Too often I label these as "mine," clinging tightly instead of using them as gifts from God to bless others. No matter the season, we're called to give generously, reflecting God's heart. Jesus assures us in Luke 6:38 that whatever we give in His name will return to us—pressed down, shaken together, and overflowing with His blessings.

How can I loosen my grip on what I've been entrusted with and offer it freely for God's glory?

_____

_____

_____

Prayer to flourish: Lord, thank You for Your greatest gift—Your Son. Please help me become more generous. I sometimes cling to what is mine and confuse stewardship with ownership. Help me to be a good steward of Your gifts. Amen.

---

1. https://www.apocryphicity.ca/2014/08/20/more-christian-apocrypha-updates-2-revelation-of-the-magi/ (accessed 3/18/25)

Good Grief?

*No eye has seen, nor ear heard, nor the heart of man imagined,
what God has prepared for those who love him.*
1 Corinthians 2:9

Many days I feel like Charlie Brown, perpetually followed by a gloomy rain cloud. When sadness overwhelmed him, he would famously groan, "Good grief." At first glance, "good" and "grief" seem like an odd pairing—two words that don't belong together. This paradox became real to me right before Christmas, when I lost my dad. Shortly after the holiday, we laid him to rest during what was the coldest week Kansas City had seen in eighty years, with wind chills plunging to -40 degrees. The bitter cold seemed to deepen the sting of an already heart-wrenching week. While I'm profoundly grateful for the promise of heaven, the ache of missing my dad remains. Grief is hard. It hurts.

My father lived a long life, for which I am thankful; yet, not all fathers have the same years. In our church family, we recently faced the heartbreaking loss of a dad who went to heaven before his son started kindergarten. Moments like this make us cry out to God, "Why?"

There's nothing that feels good about grief. And yet, the Bible offers a healing balm for grieving hearts: hope. Christ transforms our grief from hopeless to hope-filled. Just as oxygen fills our lungs, hope fills our souls. While grief is heavy, God's promises of eternal life are good. Today's Scripture reminds us that heaven is a place without grief, where goodness reigns. One day I will see my dad again and feel his warm hug. And so will you—reunited with those you love and have lost to heaven.

When does grief hit you hardest?

_____

_____

_____

Prayer to flourish: Abba Father, when grief feels heavy, making it hard to breathe, please remind me of Your promises that fill my soul with hope. I look forward to seeing You and my loved ones in heaven. Thank You for taking the *fear of death* and replacing it with the hope of heaven. Amen.

Count What Counts

> When he finally arrives, blazing in beauty and all his angels with him, the Son of Man will take his place on his glorious throne. Then all the nations will be arranged before him and he will sort the people out, much as a shepherd sorts out sheep and goats, putting sheep to his right and goats to his left.
> Matthew 25:31-33

Count what counts. In a world that counts money, steps, grams of fat, Facebook friends and Instagram followers, be different! Instead of counting things that are temporary, like calories and carbs, count your blessings then bless others out of a grateful heart.

In college I really appreciated when a professor highlighted what was most important for an exam. Jesus does the same for us when He shares what truly matters when we stand accountable for our life choices. In today's reading, He explains the six basic acts of love He'll count as if done for Him: 1) I was hungry, and you fed me. 2) I was thirsty, and you gave me a drink. 3) I was a stranger, and you invited me into your home. 4) I was naked, and you gave me clothing. 5) I was sick, and you cared for me. 6) I was in prison, and you visited me.

These acts remind us that serving "the least of these" is how we honor Christ. When we count what counts—loving others as He loves us—we live out our faith in a way that reflects His grace and compassion. This leads to a flourishing life where we can be fabulously fulfilled and confident to stand before Jesus.

Which of these six commands do you find hardest?

_____

_____

_____

Prayer to flourish: Lord, when I stand before Your mercy seat and give account of my life, I long to hear You say "Well done!" Please help me to count what counts, knowing that only faith, hope, and love last forever, and the greatest of these is love. You have blessed me so that I can bless others. Amen.

Holding Grudges or Catching Blessings

God is sheer mercy and grace; not easily angered, he's rich in love.
He doesn't endlessly nag and scold,
nor hold grudges forever.
Psalm 103:8-9 (MSG)

When we hold grudges, our hands aren't free to catch blessings. While no one knows who first said this, its truth remains undeniable. Grudges weigh us down, but letting go frees us to flourish, to see God's blessings and be a blessing to others.

Today's Bible verse reminds us that God always looks for the best in us, not the worst. His mercies are new every morning, and His amazing grace covers our imperfections. He is endlessly patient with us in every circumstance. That's the kind of spouse and friend I need—and the kind I long to be.

Forgiving and letting go of grudges isn't easy for me. It takes more than willpower; it requires supernatural help. I need The Holy Spirit dwelling in my heart, giving me the strength to release past hurts.

I'm also reminded of the gifts God freely gives: grace is the good I don't deserve while mercy is withhold the bad I do deserve. Every sunrise brings a fresh outpouring of both. With these divine gifts, I can let go of the weight of resentment and instead hold tightly to joy, remembering love and blessings that make life truly abundant.

How might letting go of a grudge today free your heart to catch more blessings?

_____

_____

_____

Prayer to flourish: Merciful Father, You are all-knowing and yet You choose not to remember our mishaps and missteps. Thank You for Your compassion and mercy each new day. Please help me to show that same kind mercy to others, letting go of grudges so I can hang onto blessings. Amen.

What's Your Giant's Name?

David replied to the Philistine, "You come to me with sword, spear, and javelin, but I come to you in the name of the Lord of Heaven's Armies—the God of the armies of Israel, whom you have defied. Today the Lord will conquer you.
1 Samuel 17:45-46a

Some people see a giant and think, *"He's so big. I can't win."* Others look at the same giant and say, *"He's so big. I can't miss!"* Giants aren't just men like Goliath who lived in the land of Gath; giants come into our lives in countless forms and sizes.

Sometimes, our Goliaths are mountains of debt or canyons of regret. For others, it's a difficult marriage or the heartbreak of a divorce. Maybe your giant is a diagnosis like diabetes or heart disease. Or perhaps it's not physical illness, but the weight of worry over a wayward child grappling with self-image or self-control. Worry itself is a formidable giant for me. It wakes me up, creeping into my dreams in the wee morning hours when I feel least equipped to fight.

Whatever form your giant takes, we can face it with the same confidence as David in today's Scripture. He boldly declared to Goliath, *"You come against me with sword and spear and javelin, but I come against you in the name of the Lord Almighty."* (1 Samuel 17:45) David knew his strength came not from himself but from God. With God, victory is assured. No giant is too big for Him to conquer and no challenge too great for His power. Like David, we can proclaim God's might and trust that He fights for us.

What giants do you need God's help to defeat?

_____

_____

_____

Prayer to flourish: Elohim, my one true God, I adore You alone. Teach me to fear (honor and respect) You more than any person who comes against me or emotion that threatens to overtake me. Thank You for Your Holy Spirit who lives within me to help me slay giants that bully my family and me. Amen.

Grace and God's Big Circle

For you are all children of God through faith in Christ Jesus. And all who have been united with Christ in baptism have put on Christ, like putting on new clothes. There is no longer Jew or Gentile, slave or free, male and female. For you are all one in Christ Jesus.
Galatians 3:26-28

My circle of friends looks a lot like me. Most are women—wives, moms, and hard workers both inside and outside their homes. They love God and their families deeply.

Today's reading made me pause and reflect on those outside my circle. God doesn't see separate circles—He draws just one, inviting everyone to step inside through faith in Christ. His circle includes the old and the young, the weak and the strong, those on the left, those on the right, and those who don't know where they fit.

God doesn't draw little, exclusive circles. No siree! Today's passage reminds us that the moment Jesus gave up His Spirit, His sacrificial death became the atonement for all of us. Through Christ, we're united as one family, clothed in His grace and love.

God's circle is wide and includes people who may annoy us. He extends His loving grace to anyone who seeks a Savior. Let's follow His example, widening our circles and inviting others into the embrace of His love.

Who do you know that needs to step inside the circle of God's loving grace through Jesus?

_____

_____

_____

Prayer to flourish: Jesus, thank You for saving me. Today I pray for ___(insert names)___ to step inside the circle of Your grace. I want to see them in eternity. Please send Your Holy Spirit to prepare their heart to hear the Good News. Help me reach out to them in both word and deed. I trust You to give me the right words. Amen.

Savor Every Season

> For everything there is a season, a time for every activity under heaven. A time to be born and a time to die. A time to plant and a time to harvest. A time to kill and a time to heal. A time to tear down and a time to build up. A time to cry and a time to laugh. A time to grieve and a time to dance.
>
> Ecclesiastes 3:1-5

What season stirs your heart? For me, it's spring—the gentle rains of April nourishing blossoms into May. Life, too, unfolds in seasons, each with its own beauty. My mom's wise words often echo in my mind: *"Savor every season. You'll blink, and your 30s will pass in a haze."* She was right. Time flows swiftly. I am grateful for each decade.

Now, I find myself in autumn's embrace. The golden leaves falling mirror the changes in my life. My children no longer cling to me as they once did, but in this season—caring for grandchildren and aging parents—contentment has taken deep root in my heart. This peace comes not from achievements or possessions but from the many gifts God has given.

I'm deeply thankful for the firm foundation my parents built, for friends whose laughter brightened my days, for nearly 40 years of shared joys and trials with my husband, and for children who walk with God, bringing Him glory and filling me with joy.

Today's reading reminds us that there is a time for everything. Life is a blend of sunshine and rain. Trials, much like rain, strengthen faith and nourish growth so we flourish. Your struggles and blessings may be different from mine, but with God's grace, we can savor every season.

What are you most anticipating in those years to come? What are you most dreading?

_____

_____

_____

Prayer to flourish: Lord, I'm grateful You are with me in the good and the bad, promising to wring and bring good from those things dripping with bad. Thank You for being beside me when I'm beside myself and distraught. Thank You for reminding me there's a time for everything. Amen.

An Excellent Ending

There was a believer in Joppa named Tabitha (which in Greek is Dorcas). She was always doing kind things for others and helping the poor. About this time she became ill and died. Her body was washed for burial and laid in an upstairs room. But the believers had heard that Peter was nearby at Lydda, so they sent two men to beg him, "Please come as soon as possible!" So Peter returned with them; and as soon as he arrived, they took him to the upstairs room. The room was filled with widows who were weeping and showing him the coats and other clothes Dorcas had made for them.

Acts 9:36-39

It seems fitting to end this devotional with an American Indian proverb that describes a flourishing life: "When you were born, you cried and the world rejoiced. Live your life so that when you die, the world cries and you rejoice."[1] Tabitha embodied this sentiment. When she died, her friends mourned deeply, showcasing her legacy of love and service.

Tabitha lived with purpose, devoting her life to running the eternal race and caring for those in need. Her life reminds us to use our gifts for God's glory, touching lives in meaningful ways.

When we were born, we cried and the world rejoiced. My prayer is that we, like Tabitha, will live so that when we die, the world will cry and we will rejoice in the presence of our Savior.

How do you most want to be remembered?

_____

_____

_____

Prayer to flourish: Elohim, You are the Alpha and the Omega, the beginning and the end. You are beside me, with me, and in me helping to write my story. Thank You for loving me during each chapter of my life. Help me to finish strong. Amen.

1. https://www.allgreatquotes.com/the-world-cries-and-you-rejoice/ (accessed 6/30/22)

About the Author

Lisa Wilt is an inspirational speaker, author of eight books, and a guest writer for Dayspring's (in)courage devotions. She is a six-time recipient of the Illumination Christian Book Awards which honor the year's best new titles written and published with a Christian worldview.

Lisa's 1-Minute WOW Words airs daily on the radio to lighten the load for those on the go and can be found on all podcast platforms. She is founder of *Lisa Wilt Ministries*. Visit her at LisaWilt.com.

For over 34 years Lisa worked full time as an award-winning pharmacist in community pharmacy and the pharmaceutical industry. By grace, Lisa and her husband have two grown children who have followed in their medical footpaths. Of all her accomplishments, the title that most defines Lisa is *child of God*. As her family will tell you, she likes pickles and dislikes being pickled when playing Pickleball.

Leave a Review & Enjoy Other Books

Please scan below to leave a much-appreciated review and help others find JOY in Jesus. If you would like to become a valued member of my future Launch Teams, reach out to me at LisaWilt.com.

- **Turn Over A New Leaf:** 70 Relatable Devotions for Abundant Living
- **Windows of Wonder**: Discovering Extraordinary W.O.W. Moments in the Ordinary
- **Always Uplifting**: A Daily Devotion to Lighten Your Load
- **You're Invited To The Table**: A Royal Story of Love
- **Delight Drizzled Days**: Sweet Devotions for Abundant Living

Made in the USA
Monee, IL
11 April 2025

15586899R00085